Machine Learning Made Simple

Master AI Algorithms Without Complex Math A Beginner-Friendly Approach to Data Science, Predictive Modeling, and Deep Learning

Greyson Chesterfield

RIGHT

DISCLAIMER

The information provided in this book is for general informational purposes only. All content in this book reflects the author's views and is based on their research, knowledge, and experiences. The author and publisher make no representations or warranties of any kind concerning the completeness, accuracy, reliability, suitability, or availability of the information contained herein.

This book is not intended to be a substitute for professional advice, diagnosis, or treatment. Readers should seek professional advice for any specific concerns or conditions. The author and publisher disclaim any liability or responsibility for any direct, indirect, incidental, or consequential loss or damage arising from the use of the information contained in this book.

Chapter 1: Welcome to the World of Machine Learning

Introduction

Machine Learning (ML) isn't just a buzzword anymore—it's a transformative technology that's reshaping the way we interact with the world around us. From predicting what movie to watch next to detecting fraudulent transactions, machine learning is quietly embedded into almost every aspect of modern life. But what exactly is machine learning, and why should you care about it?

In this chapter, we'll dive into the basics of machine learning, how it differs from artificial intelligence (AI) and deep learning (DL), and why it's more accessible than you might think—even if you don't have a Ph.D. in mathematics.

What is Machine Learning?

At its core, **machine learning** is a subset of artificial intelligence (AI) that focuses on developing algorithms that allow computers to learn from and make predictions or decisions based on data. It's a field of computer science that enables systems to **learn from experience**—without being explicitly programmed to do so.

For example, when you watch Netflix and it recommends shows based on your previous viewing habits, that recommendation engine is powered by machine learning. It learns what types of shows you enjoy watching and suggests similar titles. It's not magic; it's just data and math working in the background to make your experience better.

Machine learning works by feeding large amounts of data into algorithms. These algorithms process the data, identifying patterns and making predictions or decisions based on those patterns. Over time, as more data is fed into the system, the algorithm "learns" from the data, continuously improving its accuracy and performance.

Here's a simplified breakdown:

- **Input**: Data (e.g., historical data on movie ratings, customer purchase behavior, or medical records)

- **Processing**: The algorithm analyzes the data to find patterns, correlations, or trends.

- **Output**: Predictions or actions based on the learned patterns (e.g., movie recommendations, fraud detection, or medical diagnoses).

What's interesting about machine learning is that it can handle tasks too complex for traditional programming. Rather than coding specific rules, machine learning allows a system to identify patterns on its own.

AI, Machine Learning, and Deep Learning – What's the Difference?

Before we dive deeper into machine learning, let's take a moment to clarify the terms AI, machine learning, and deep learning. While the terms are often used interchangeably, they refer to distinct concepts, and it's essential to understand their relationship.

- **Artificial Intelligence (AI)** is the broadest term. It refers to the simulation of human intelligence in machines that are programmed to think, learn, and problem-solve. AI systems can be rule-based, expert systems, or even something like a chess program that uses predefined rules to make decisions. AI doesn't always have to "learn" from data; it can be programmed to perform specific tasks based on hardcoded rules.

- **Machine Learning (ML)**, as mentioned earlier, is a subset of AI. It's the part of AI that focuses on learning from data. Rather than being programmed with explicit instructions, an ML system is trained on data and uses statistical methods to find patterns and make predictions. This is where the magic of modern AI happens, as it enables machines to improve their behavior over time based on new data.

- **Deep Learning (DL)** is a more specific subset of machine learning that uses neural networks with many layers (hence the term "deep") to analyze large amounts of data. Deep learning is responsible for much of the recent success in AI, including things like image recognition, speech recognition, and natural language processing (NLP). It requires massive amounts of data and computational power but has led to breakthroughs in various industries.

In simple terms:

- **AI** is the broader goal of autonomous machines.

- **ML** is a way to achieve AI by learning from data.

- **DL** is a specialized approach within ML that uses complex neural networks to process data.

As a beginner, it's essential to focus on machine learning, which offers a more accessible entry point compared to deep learning's advanced methods. Deep learning, while powerful, is often more resource-intensive and requires knowledge of neural networks and a solid understanding of math.

Why is Machine Learning Accessible to Everyone?

One of the most exciting aspects of machine learning is that **it doesn't require advanced mathematics** to get started. Sure, math is involved at a higher level, but you don't need to be a math expert to begin experimenting with machine learning. Thanks to the rise of open-source libraries like **scikit-learn**, **TensorFlow**, and **PyTorch**, it's easier than ever for beginners to start implementing machine learning models without worrying about the complex math behind the scenes.

Let's break it down:

1. **Pre-built Algorithms**: Libraries like scikit-learn, TensorFlow, and PyTorch provide pre-built algorithms that you can use directly without needing to understand all the underlying equations. These libraries abstract away the math so you can focus on solving real-world problems.

2. **Step-by-Step Tutorials**: Today, you can find countless tutorials and documentation that

guide you through machine learning processes step by step. These resources are designed for beginners and provide hands-on experience rather than diving straight into theory-heavy content.

3. **Community Support**: Machine learning has one of the most active and supportive communities. If you encounter an issue or don't understand something, a quick search will usually lead you to an answer. There are forums like Stack Overflow, GitHub, and specialized communities like Kaggle where you can learn from others' experiences.

4. **Learning by Doing**: Machine learning is one of those fields where you can get started with simple projects and build your way up. You don't need to understand all the deep theoretical concepts right away. The best way to learn is by doing. As you experiment and solve real problems, you'll naturally pick up the concepts and techniques you need to know.

5. **Tools That Do the Heavy Lifting**: With tools like Jupyter notebooks, Google Colab, and various cloud-based services, you don't even need

powerful hardware to start learning. You can run machine learning experiments on cloud servers, and these platforms often come with pre-configured environments, making it easy for you to get started quickly.

Machine learning is becoming more user-friendly and accessible to anyone with curiosity and persistence. Whether you're a hobbyist, a professional looking to upskill, or a student wanting to explore the world of AI, the tools and resources are available for you to start experimenting and learning right now.

Real-World Examples of Machine Learning in Action

Machine learning is already having a massive impact on the world, and it's likely that you've interacted with machine learning systems in your everyday life. Let's look at a few practical examples that highlight how ML is improving various aspects of daily life.

1. Recommendation Systems (Netflix, YouTube, Amazon)

We all know the frustration of not knowing what to watch on Netflix or YouTube. That's where machine learning comes in. Platforms like Netflix and YouTube use **recommendation systems** powered by machine learning to suggest content based on your viewing history and preferences.

For example:

- Netflix analyzes the movies or TV shows you've watched, the ratings you've given, and the time you spend watching certain genres. It then uses this data to recommend similar content you might enjoy.

- YouTube's recommendation algorithm works in a similar way. It looks at the videos you've watched, the channels you're subscribed to, and even your comments and likes, then suggests videos it thinks you'll enjoy.

These systems use machine learning techniques like **collaborative filtering** and **content-based filtering** to find patterns in your behavior and suggest content that's most likely to interest you.

2. Spam Filters in Email

How many times have you checked your inbox only to find that an important email was sent to the spam folder? Or, maybe your inbox has been surprisingly spam-free despite the occasional sketchy email address.

That's machine learning at work.

Spam filters use algorithms that **learn** to identify spam based on patterns in emails. Initially, the system may rely on basic rules (e.g., certain keywords like "free," "buy now," or "limited offer"). However, over time, the filter becomes smarter by learning from your interactions. If you mark an email as spam, the system takes note of that behavior, improving its ability to classify future emails as either spam or legitimate.

This is a perfect example of **supervised learning**, where the model is trained on labeled data (emails marked as spam or not spam) and then used to classify new emails.

3. Fraud Detection in Banking

Machine learning plays a critical role in detecting fraudulent activity in banks and financial institutions. Systems use transaction data to create a profile of what constitutes **normal behavior** for a given customer.

- If you suddenly make a large purchase in another country, the system may flag this as suspicious and ask for verification before processing the transaction.

- ML models continuously update based on new patterns they observe, which means they get better over time at distinguishing legitimate transactions from fraudulent ones.

This involves techniques like **anomaly detection**, where the system flags anything outside of normal patterns as potentially fraudulent.

4. Self-Driving Cars

While still in development, **self-driving cars** are one of the most exciting applications of machine learning. These cars use machine learning algorithms to make decisions based on data from sensors, cameras, and other sources. The algorithms help the car understand its environment, make predictions about what other drivers might do, and navigate safely from one place to another.

This involves deep learning and neural networks to process vast amounts of sensory data and make real-time decisions. It's an example of how machine learning can be used in highly dynamic and real-time situations.

Hands-On Project Idea: Running Your First ML Script

Now that we've covered what machine learning is and some real-world examples, it's time to **get your hands dirty** and run your first machine learning script. Don't worry—it's not complicated.

Project: A Simple Classifier Using scikit-learn

We'll use a tiny dataset and build a basic **classifier** using the Python library **scikit-learn**. A classifier is a type of machine learning model that categorizes data into different groups.

Step 1: Install Required Libraries

To get started, you'll need to install Python and some essential libraries. You can do this by running the following commands in your terminal:

bash

pip install numpy pandas scikit-learn matplotlib

Step 2: Import the Libraries

Start by importing the libraries we'll need for this project.

python

```
import numpy as np

import pandas as pd

from sklearn.model_selection import train_test_split

from sklearn.neighbors import KNeighborsClassifier

from sklearn.metrics import accuracy_score
```

Step 3: Load the Dataset

For simplicity, we'll use the **Iris dataset,** which contains information about different types of flowers. This dataset is built into scikit-learn, so we don't need to download it.

python

```
from sklearn.datasets import load_iris

iris = load_iris()
```

data = iris.data

labels = iris.target

Step 4: Split the Data

Next, we'll split the dataset into two parts: training and testing data.

python

X_train, X_test, y_train, y_test = train_test_split(data, labels, test_size=0.2)

Step 5: Create the Classifier

Now, we'll use a **K-Nearest Neighbors (KNN)** classifier. This is a simple, intuitive model that classifies data points based on their proximity to other points.

python

model = KNeighborsClassifier()

model.fit(X_train, y_train)

Step 6: Make Predictions

Now that the model is trained, we can use it to predict the labels for the test data.

python

```
predictions = model.predict(X_test)
```

Step 7: Evaluate the Model

Finally, we'll evaluate the model's accuracy by comparing its predictions to the actual labels.

python

```
print(f'Accuracy: {accuracy_score(y_test, predictions)}')
```

Congratulations! You've just run your first machine learning script, and you've trained a model to classify flowers based on certain features. You can now experiment with other datasets and try different algorithms.

Encouragement & Mindset

It's common to feel overwhelmed when you first dive into machine learning, but remember: **curiosity is more important than expertise**. No one starts as an expert, and the beauty of machine learning is that it's a field where you can learn through hands-on experimentation.

The more you practice, the better you'll become. Even small projects, like the one you just completed, add up over time and deepen your understanding of the field. It's all about **consistency**—the more you explore and experiment, the more natural the concepts will become.

So don't worry about getting everything perfect right away. Instead, focus on **learning by doing**. Machine learning is a field that rewards persistence and curiosity. And as long as you keep exploring and practicing, you'll be on the path to mastering the fundamentals and moving on to more advanced topics.

Summary

In this chapter, we've introduced the exciting world of machine learning, covering the basics of what it is, how it differs from AI and deep learning, and why it's accessible to anyone willing to put in the effort. We've explored some real-world applications of machine learning in everyday life, from movie recommendations to spam filters and fraud detection.

With your first hands-on project complete, you've gained practical experience in using machine learning to solve a simple classification problem. Now that you have the foundational knowledge, you're ready to dive deeper into the world of machine learning and tackle more complex projects. The key to success in machine learning is to stay curious and keep practicing, and as you progress, you'll develop the skills and confidence to build your own intelligent systems.

Chapter 2: Setting Up Your Environment

Introduction

Setting up the right environment for machine learning is crucial for ensuring that your development process is smooth and efficient. Before you dive into creating models and analyzing data, you need to ensure that you have the right tools and libraries in place.

This chapter will guide you step-by-step through the process of setting up a Python environment for machine learning, installing essential libraries, and getting familiar with the tools you will use regularly in the field. You'll learn how to install and configure Python, set up libraries like **NumPy, pandas, scikit-learn**, and **TensorFlow/PyTorch**, and also get comfortable using **Jupyter Notebooks** or your preferred code editor.

By the end of this chapter, you'll have your own personalized environment ready for experimentation and data science projects.

Why Python for Machine Learning?

Python has become the go-to language for machine learning for several reasons:

1. **Simplicity and Readability**: Python's simple, human-readable syntax allows you to focus on solving problems rather than dealing with complex language syntax.

2. **Vast Ecosystem**: Python has a rich ecosystem of libraries, frameworks, and tools that make machine learning development easier and faster. Libraries like **NumPy, pandas, scikit-learn, TensorFlow**, and **PyTorch** provide pre-built algorithms and tools for data manipulation, model building, and optimization.

3. **Community and Documentation**: Python has one of the largest and most supportive communities in the data science field. You can find tutorials, guides, and community-driven

content for virtually every aspect of machine learning development.

4. **Versatility**: Python is used across a wide range of fields, from web development to scientific computing and artificial intelligence. This versatility makes it an excellent choice for anyone starting out in machine learning.

In the next section, we'll get hands-on with installing Python and setting up the necessary tools for your machine learning journey.

Installing Python and Essential Libraries

The first step to building a machine learning environment is installing Python. Don't worry; the process is relatively straightforward, and we'll guide you through it step by step.

Installing Python

Python can be downloaded from the official Python website: https://www.python.org/downloads/.

1. **Download the Python Installer**: Visit the download page and select the appropriate version for your operating system (Windows,

macOS, or Linux). The latest stable version should work fine, but make sure it's **Python 3.x** (as Python 2.x is no longer supported).

2. **Running the Installer (Windows):**

   - Once the installer is downloaded, open it and make sure to check the box labeled **Add Python to PATH** before clicking **Install Now**. This step is essential because it makes Python accessible from the command line.

   - After the installation is complete, you can verify that Python is installed correctly by opening the Command Prompt and typing:

bash

python --version

   - If Python was installed correctly, you should see the Python version number.

3. **Running the Installer (macOS/Linux):**

- For **macOS**, Python comes pre-installed. However, it's often an older version. You can update it using **Homebrew** (a package manager for macOS):

bash

brew install python

- For **Linux** (Ubuntu/Debian), you can use the following command:

bash

sudo apt update

sudo apt install python3

Once Python is installed, it's time to set up a package manager called **pip**, which is used to install Python libraries.

Installing Essential Libraries

Machine learning relies heavily on libraries for numerical computation, data manipulation, and model building. Below are the essential libraries you will need for your machine learning setup.

1. **NumPy**: NumPy is the core library for numerical computing in Python. It provides support for arrays, matrices, and many mathematical functions.

2. **pandas**: pandas is a powerful library used for data manipulation and analysis. It provides data structures like DataFrames that allow you to work efficiently with large datasets.

3. **scikit-learn**: scikit-learn is one of the most popular libraries for machine learning in Python. It provides simple and efficient tools for data mining and data analysis. It includes algorithms for classification, regression, clustering, and model selection.

4. **TensorFlow/PyTorch**: These two libraries are essential for deep learning and building more complex models. TensorFlow is developed by Google, and PyTorch is developed by Facebook. Both are widely used in industry for building deep learning models.

To install these libraries, you can use **pip**, the package installer for Python. In your terminal or command prompt, run the following commands:

bash

pip install numpy pandas scikit-learn

pip install tensorflow # For TensorFlow (alternative: pip install torch for PyTorch)

It's often a good idea to install these libraries in a **virtual environment** to isolate project dependencies and avoid version conflicts.

Setting Up a Virtual Environment

A virtual environment is a self-contained directory that contains everything needed to run a Python project, including Python executables, libraries, and other dependencies. This is useful because it allows you to manage dependencies on a per-project basis.

Here's how you can set up a virtual environment:

1. **Install virtualenv**: If you don't have **virtualenv** installed, you can install it via pip:

bash

pip install virtualenv

2. **Create a Virtual Environment**: Navigate to your project folder and run the following command:

bash

virtualenv myenv

This creates a new directory called **myenv** containing the isolated environment.

3. **Activate the Virtual Environment**: To activate the environment, use the following commands depending on your operating system:

   o **Windows:**

bash

.\myenv\Scripts\activate

   o **macOS/Linux:**

bash

source myenv/bin/activate

4. You'll see the environment name in parentheses in your terminal, indicating that it's active.

5. **Deactivate the Virtual Environment**: To deactivate the environment when you're done working on your project, simply run:

bash

deactivate

Using a virtual environment ensures that your machine learning project has the correct dependencies and versions, avoiding conflicts with other Python projects.

Installing Jupyter Notebooks

While you can use any code editor to write Python code, **Jupyter Notebooks** is an incredibly useful tool for data science and machine learning. It allows you to write and run Python code in small, manageable chunks and view outputs directly alongside your code.

To install Jupyter, simply run:

bash

```
pip install notebook
```

After the installation is complete, you can start a Jupyter notebook by running:

bash

```
jupyter notebook
```

This command will open the Jupyter Notebook interface in your web browser, where you can create and manage notebooks. Each notebook consists of cells that can contain code, markdown text, and visualizations.

Code Editors: PyCharm vs. VS Code

While Jupyter is great for experimentation, you'll likely want to use a full-featured code editor or Integrated

Development Environment (IDE) for larger projects. Here are two popular options for Python development:

1. **PyCharm**:

   o PyCharm is a powerful IDE specifically designed for Python development. It offers features like intelligent code completion, debugging, and project management.

   o You can download PyCharm from https://www.jetbrains.com/pycharm/.

2. **Visual Studio Code (VS Code)**:

   o VS Code is a lightweight and highly customizable code editor that is popular among data scientists and developers alike. It supports Python through extensions and can be configured for machine learning development.

   o You can download VS Code from https://code.visualstudio.com/.

Both editors support Jupyter Notebooks as well, so you can choose whichever suits your workflow.

Basic Command-Line Skills for Data Science Projects

The command line is an essential tool for data science and machine learning. It allows you to quickly navigate your file system, install libraries, run scripts, and manage virtual environments. Here are some basic commands that will be helpful:

1. **Navigating the File System**:

   - **Change directory**: cd directory_name

   - **List files in the current directory**: ls (macOS/Linux), dir (Windows)

   - **Create a new directory**: mkdir new_directory

   - **Delete a file**: rm file_name (macOS/Linux), del file_name (Windows)

2. **Running Python Scripts**:

   - To run a Python script, navigate to the directory containing the script and run:

bash

python script_name.py

3. **Installing Packages**:

   ○ You can install Python packages directly
   from the command line using pip:

bash

pip install package_name

4. **Listing Installed Packages**:

   ○ To list all the installed Python packages,
   use:

bash

pip list

Hands-On Project: Creating a Simple Data Analysis Notebook

Now that your environment is set up, it's time to get hands-on. Let's walk through a simple data analysis project using Jupyter Notebooks.

1. **Create a New Notebook:**

   o Open your terminal, navigate to the directory where you want to create the notebook, and run:

bash

jupyter notebook

   o This will open a browser window. From there, you can create a new notebook by clicking **New** and selecting **Python 3**.

2. **Loading a Dataset:** Let's load a sample dataset. We'll use **pandas** to load a CSV file into a DataFrame. For this project, we'll use a dataset of used car sales.

Start by running this code in the first cell:

python

import pandas as pd

 # Load dataset

```python
data = pd.read_csv("used_cars.csv")
```

```python
# Display the first 5 rows
data.head()
```

3. **Exploring the Data**: Next, let's explore the data by displaying summary statistics and checking for missing values.

python

```python
# Display summary statistics
data.describe()
```

```python
# Check for missing values
data.isnull().sum()
```

4. **Data Visualization**: Let's visualize some of the data. We'll use **matplotlib** for plotting.

python

```python
import matplotlib.pyplot as plt
```

```
# Plot distribution of car prices

plt.hist(data['price'], bins=50)

plt.title("Distribution of Car Prices")

plt.xlabel("Price")

plt.ylabel("Frequency")

plt.show()
```

5. **Basic Data Analysis**: Finally, let's analyze the relationship between car mileage and price.

python

```
# Scatter plot of mileage vs price

plt.scatter(data['mileage'], data['price'])

plt.title("Mileage vs Price")

plt.xlabel("Mileage")

plt.ylabel("Price")

plt.show()
```

This hands-on project gives you the opportunity to practice loading data, exploring it, and visualizing key features. It's a simple but effective introduction to data analysis in Python.

Conclusion

In this chapter, we've set up your environment for machine learning and data science. From installing Python and key libraries like **NumPy, pandas, scikit-learn**, and **TensorFlow/PyTorch** to setting up a virtual environment and starting Jupyter Notebooks, you now have the tools to start experimenting with data.

With your environment ready and your first data analysis project completed, you're now prepared to dive deeper into the world of machine learning. The next step is to start experimenting with real datasets and building your own models. The possibilities are endless, and you're off to a great start!

Chapter 3: Understanding Data – The Heart of Machine Learning

Introduction

In the world of machine learning (ML), **data is everything**. The success of your machine learning model is entirely dependent on the quality of the data you feed it. Whether you're predicting trends in stock prices, diagnosing diseases in healthcare, or recommending products in retail, the underlying data is the backbone of all machine learning systems. To make the most of ML algorithms, understanding data is key.

This chapter is dedicated to helping you **understand data**, with a focus on recognizing different data types, grasping the basics of statistics (without diving too deep into the math), and realizing the importance of data cleaning. Data cleaning can often take more time than building models, but it's a critical step that directly impacts the accuracy of your results.

In addition to this, we'll walk through practical examples and guide you through a hands-on project using a messy dataset—an essential skill every data scientist must develop. By the end of this chapter, you will have a strong foundation to start working with data in a meaningful way, making sure it's ready for machine learning models to process.

Types of Data: Structured vs. Unstructured, Categorical vs. Numerical

Before we dive into working with data, it's essential to understand **the different types of data** you'll encounter. Machine learning models behave very differently based on the type of data they're dealing with, so recognizing these distinctions will guide how you handle, preprocess, and model your data.

Structured Data:

Structured data is organized in a **tabular format,** meaning it fits neatly into rows and columns, much like a spreadsheet or a database table. Each column represents a feature (e.g., "Age," "Price," "Height"), and each row represents an observation or record. Structured data is often easy to analyze because of its clear format, making it the most common type of data used in machine learning tasks.

- **Examples of Structured Data:**

  o **Healthcare Data:** Patient information like age, weight, blood pressure, and test results.

  o **Retail Transactions:** Product details (name, price, quantity), customer information, and transaction dates.

  o **Financial Data:** Stock prices, sales figures, and customer transactions.

Structured data typically comes from databases, CSV files, or spreadsheets, making it relatively easy to load into memory and process using libraries like **pandas** in Python.

Unstructured Data:

Unstructured data is the **wild west** of data. It doesn't fit neatly into rows and columns and is much harder to organize. Examples of unstructured data include free-form text, images, audio, and video. To use unstructured data in machine learning, it usually needs to be **preprocessed** into a structured format.

- **Examples of Unstructured Data**:
    - **Text**: Email messages, social media posts, news articles.
    - **Images**: Photos, medical scans, screenshots.
    - **Audio**: Voice recordings, podcasts, sound clips.

To handle unstructured data, techniques like **Natural Language Processing (NLP)** for text or **Convolutional Neural Networks (CNNs)** for images are typically used. These fields require more advanced techniques compared to structured data but are crucial for tasks like speech recognition, image classification, and sentiment analysis.

Categorical vs. Numerical Data:

Data can be further classified into **categorical** and **numerical** types, which will determine how you handle and analyze the data.

Categorical Data:

Categorical data consists of values that represent categories or groups. These values are often non-numerical, though they may be represented as numbers for convenience. The key characteristic of categorical data is that the numbers themselves don't have mathematical significance (i.e., they cannot be added, subtracted, or averaged).

- **Types of Categorical Data:**
  - **Nominal:** Categories with no inherent order. Examples: colors (red, blue, green), gender (male, female), or country of origin.

  - **Ordinal:** Categories with a defined order or ranking, but without a consistent scale. Examples: customer satisfaction ratings (low, medium, high), education levels (high school, undergraduate, graduate).

Numerical Data:

Numerical data consists of numbers and represents measurable quantities. This data can be analyzed mathematically, meaning you can perform operations like addition, subtraction, and averaging. Numerical data can be broken down into two subcategories:

- **Discrete**: Values that are distinct and countable. Examples: number of children, number of products sold.

- **Continuous**: Values that are continuous and can take on an infinite number of values within a range. Examples: height, weight, temperature.

In machine learning, **numerical data** is often used to calculate key performance metrics, and it plays a crucial role in model building.

Basic Statistics: Mean, Median, Standard Deviation

In machine learning, you need to understand **basic statistics** to summarize and describe your data. These statistical measures help you get a feel for the data and are the foundation for much of the data exploration you'll do in the early stages of a project.

Mean:

The **mean**, or **average**, is the sum of all values divided by the number of values. It gives you an overall sense of the "central" value of a dataset.

- **Formula**:

$$\text{Mean} = \frac{\sum \text{values}}{n}$$

Where n is the number of values.

- **Example**: If you're analyzing the prices of a set of products, the mean price is calculated by adding all prices and dividing by the number of products.

Median:

The **median** is the middle value in a dataset when the values are sorted in ascending or descending order. If there's an even number of data points, the median is the average of the two middle values. The median is useful because it is **not affected by extreme values** (outliers), making it a more reliable measure of central tendency when your data is skewed.

- **Example**: If you have the values: [1, 2, 3, 4, 100], the **mean** would be 22, but the **median** would be 3. This illustrates how the median can be a more accurate representation of the "typical" value when outliers are present.

Standard Deviation (SD):

The **standard deviation** measures the spread or dispersion of data around the mean. A high standard deviation indicates that the data points are spread out over a wider range, while a low standard deviation indicates that the data points are close to the mean.

- **Formula**:

Standard Deviation=∑(xi−μ)2n\text{Standard Deviation} = \sqrt{\frac{\sum (x_i - \mu)^2}{n}}Standard Deviation=n∑(xi−μ)2

Where xix_ixi is each individual data point and μ\muμ is the mean of the dataset.

- **Example**: If you're analyzing the heights of a group of people and find that most of them are around 5'8", the standard deviation will be low. If some people are 4'10" and others are 6'4", the standard deviation will be higher, reflecting more variability in the data.

Why These Metrics Matter in Machine Learning:

When working with machine learning models, it's important to understand how your data is distributed. For example:

- Knowing the **mean** and **median** helps you determine if your data is **skewed**, which could affect the performance of certain algorithms.

- **Standard deviation** tells you if your data points are tightly clustered or widely spread, influencing model choices, especially for algorithms like **k-nearest neighbors** (KNN) and **linear regression**.

These basic statistical measures provide the necessary intuition to understand the shape of your data and guide how you preprocess and model it.

The Importance of Cleaning Data

While data may look neat at first glance, in reality, it's often **messy**. Data cleaning is one of the most crucial steps in any machine learning project because, without clean data, your model won't perform well— even if you choose the best algorithm.

Common Data Cleaning Tasks:

1. **Handling Missing Values**: Missing data is a common issue in real-world datasets. There are several ways to deal with missing values:

   o **Remove** rows or columns with missing data, but this should only be done if the missing values are a small percentage of the data.

   o **Impute** missing values with the mean, median, or mode, depending on the type of data.

   o **Use advanced techniques** like **KNN imputation**, which uses the values of similar data points to estimate missing values.

2. **Handling Duplicates**: Duplicates in the dataset can cause bias in your models and affect performance. Removing duplicates ensures that each data point is unique and represents a single observation.

3. **Outlier Detection and Removal**: Outliers are data points that are significantly different from others. While they may be genuine, they can

distort statistical analyses and machine learning models. Identifying and handling outliers is an essential part of data cleaning.

4. **Data Transformation**: Sometimes, you need to transform your data into a different format. This could mean normalizing or scaling numerical data to bring all features into the same range, or encoding categorical variables (e.g., converting "Male" and "Female" into binary 0 and 1).

5. **Data Standardization**: For algorithms like **k-means clustering** or **SVM**, data standardization is important. Standardization ensures that all features contribute equally to the model's decision, preventing certain features from dominating due to their larger scale.

Real-World Applications of Data in Machine Learning

Machine learning is used extensively in various industries, and the type of data used can vary widely depending on the domain. Let's look at a few key sectors where data plays a pivotal role in machine learning applications.

Healthcare Data (Patient Records)

In healthcare, machine learning algorithms are used to predict patient outcomes, diagnose diseases, and personalize treatment plans. This relies on large datasets of **patient records**, including vital signs, lab results, medical history, and more. Cleaning and preprocessing this data are crucial steps to ensure the model can make accurate predictions.

- **Example**: Predicting whether a patient will develop a certain condition based on their medical history and lifestyle choices. Missing data in these records could lead to incorrect predictions, and duplicate entries can distort the analysis.

Sales Data (Retail Transactions)

In retail, machine learning models are applied to sales data to predict demand, optimize pricing, and recommend products. **Sales transactions** often come with several features like customer demographics, product categories, quantities purchased, and purchase history.

- **Example**: A model trained on historical sales data can help predict future demand for products, optimizing inventory and minimizing waste. Cleaning this data ensures that the predictions are based on valid, up-to-date information.

Hands-On Project: Clean and Explore a Messy Dataset

Now that you understand the importance of clean data, let's apply this knowledge to a hands-on project. We'll clean and explore a publicly available dataset (we'll use a small subset of the **Titanic** or **Iris** dataset) and show how each cleaning step directly affects machine learning outcomes.

Step 1: Load the Dataset

First, we'll load the Titanic dataset into a pandas DataFrame:

python

import pandas as pd

 # Load the Titanic dataset

```
data = pd.read_csv("titanic.csv")
```

```
# Display the first 5 rows
```

```
data.head()
```

Step 2: Identify Missing Values

Check for missing values in the dataset:

```
python
```

```
# Check for missing values
```

```
data.isnull().sum()
```

If we find missing values in important columns like **Age**, we might want to impute the missing values with the **mean** or **median** for numerical features, or with the **mode** for categorical features.

Step 3: Remove Duplicates

Next, we'll check for duplicate rows and remove them:

```
python
```

 # Remove duplicate rows

data = data.drop_duplicates()

Step 4: Handle Outliers

We can detect outliers by looking at the **Age** and **Fare** columns, where values that are too high or too low could be unrealistic:

python

 # Identify outliers in Age and Fare columns

import matplotlib.pyplot as plt

data['Age'].plot(kind='box')

plt.show()

data['Fare'].plot(kind='box')

plt.show()

Step 5: Transform Data

For categorical data like **Sex**, we can encode it into numeric values (e.g., Male = 0, Female = 1):

python

```
# Encode 'Sex' column into numeric values
data['Sex'] = data['Sex'].map({'male': 0, 'female': 1})
```

Conclusion

Understanding data is a critical first step in any machine learning project. By mastering the concepts of structured vs. unstructured data, categorical vs. numerical data, and basic statistical measures, you're building the foundation for successful model creation.

Equally important is the skill of **data cleaning**. In the real world, data is messy, and cleaning it properly can significantly impact your model's performance. Through hands-on practice, you've learned how to handle missing values, duplicates, outliers, and data transformations—skills that will be vital as you move forward in machine learning.

As you work with increasingly complex datasets, remember: **garbage in, garbage out**. The quality of your data directly affects the success of your machine learning project, so make sure it's in the best shape possible before feeding it into your models.

Chapter 4: From Data to Insights – Exploratory Data Analysis (EDA)

Introduction

In machine learning, the journey from raw data to actionable insights is paved by **Exploratory Data Analysis (EDA)**. This crucial step helps you to understand the underlying patterns in your data before diving into model building. EDA allows you to form hypotheses about the relationships between variables, identify data issues (such as missing values or outliers), and explore trends that can guide further analysis or feature engineering. It is a necessary bridge between **data collection** and **model training**, and it forms the foundation of any data-driven decision-making process.

This chapter will focus on the tools and techniques used in **EDA,** including data visualization (e.g., histograms, scatter plots, box plots), data transformation (normalization, scaling), and how to identify correlations and patterns. Through practical examples and a hands-on project, you'll learn how to transform raw data into valuable insights that can guide your machine learning models.

What is Exploratory Data Analysis (EDA)?

Exploratory Data Analysis (EDA) is the process of analyzing datasets to summarize their main characteristics, often with visual methods. The goal of EDA is not just to summarize the data but to uncover hidden patterns, spot anomalies, test hypotheses, and check assumptions through the use of statistical graphics, plots, and other data visualization methods.

EDA is an iterative process where you continuously dive deeper into the data, refining your understanding of the problem and deciding which features to include in your models.

Key EDA Techniques

EDA involves a mix of visualizations, summary statistics, and transformations to understand the data's structure and relationships. In this section, we'll cover the **core techniques** that you'll frequently use to explore your data.

1. Visualizing Data:

Visualization is one of the most powerful tools in a data scientist's toolkit. It helps transform complex numerical data into visual forms, which can be much easier to understand. By visualizing data, you can see patterns, trends, outliers, and correlations that may not be obvious in the raw data.

Let's break down some of the most common types of visualizations used in EDA:

Histograms:

A **histogram** is a type of bar chart that shows the distribution of a numerical variable. It divides the data into bins and counts how many data points fall into each bin. Histograms are great for understanding the **distribution** of a single feature.

- **Use Cases:**

  - Checking the distribution of values (e.g., age, income, product prices).

  - Identifying skewness in data (left-skewed or right-skewed).

- **Example:** Suppose you're analyzing a dataset of house prices. A histogram will show you whether most houses are priced in the lower range or if there are outliers in the higher price range.

Box Plots:

A **box plot** (or **box-and-whisker plot**) displays the distribution of data based on **five summary statistics**: minimum, first quartile (Q1), median, third quartile (Q3), and maximum. The "whiskers" represent the range of the data, while the box represents the interquartile range (IQR). Box plots are excellent for detecting outliers.

- **Use Cases:**

  - Identifying outliers.

- o Comparing distributions across different categories (e.g., house prices by neighborhood).

- **Example**: You might use a box plot to compare the distribution of house prices across different cities, helping you understand where the price range is wider and where the data is more concentrated.

Scatter Plots:

A **scatter plot** is used to show the relationship between two numerical variables. It plots individual data points on a two-dimensional graph, with one variable on the X-axis and the other on the Y-axis. Scatter plots are great for detecting **correlations** and outliers.

- **Use Cases**:

    - o Analyzing relationships between two numerical features (e.g., age vs. income, height vs. weight).

    - o Detecting linear or non-linear relationships between variables.

- **Example**: A scatter plot of **square footage** vs. **price** can help you visualize the correlation between the size of a house and its market price.

Pair Plots:

A **pair plot** visualizes relationships between multiple numerical features simultaneously. It creates scatter plots for each combination of features and histograms along the diagonal to visualize the distribution of each feature. Pair plots are particularly useful for multivariate analysis.

- **Use Cases:**

  - Exploring the relationship between several numerical variables at once.

  - Detecting correlations and clustering of data points.

- **Example**: A pair plot of features like **square footage, number of bedrooms**, and **price** can help you see how these features correlate with each other.

2. Identifying Patterns and Correlations:

Once you've visualized your data, the next step is to **identify relationships** between variables. These relationships can offer insights into which features may be useful for prediction tasks.

Correlation:

The correlation between two variables measures the **strength and direction** of their relationship. The most common way to calculate correlation is through the **Pearson correlation coefficient**, which ranges from -1 to 1. A positive correlation (close to 1) means that as one variable increases, the other also increases. A negative correlation (close to -1) means that as one variable increases, the other decreases. A correlation close to 0 suggests no linear relationship.

- **Use Cases**:
    - Understanding which features are strongly related and might be useful predictors.

    - Identifying redundant features that convey similar information.

- **Example**: In a housing price dataset, you might find a strong positive correlation between **square footage** and **price**, meaning larger houses tend to cost more. You might also find a negative correlation between **age of the house** and **price**, meaning older houses tend to be cheaper.

Correlation Matrix:

A **correlation matrix** is a table that shows the correlation coefficients between many variables. It's a quick way to identify relationships between multiple features and understand which variables may be highly correlated.

- **Use Cases**:
  - Determining which features are correlated with each other.
  - Finding potential multicollinearity issues, where two or more features are highly correlated, which can impact model performance.
- **Example**: A correlation matrix for a housing dataset might show that **price** is highly

correlated with **square footage** and **number of bedrooms**, but less so with **year built**.

3. Data Transformations: Normalization and Scaling:

In machine learning, **scaling** and **normalizing** the data are critical steps to ensure that models perform optimally. Data transformations adjust the range of numerical values to allow the model to better understand the relationships between variables.

Normalization:

Normalization, or **min-max scaling**, adjusts the values of numeric columns to fit within a specific range (usually 0 to 1). This is particularly important when using algorithms like **k-nearest neighbors (KNN)** or **neural networks**, which are sensitive to the scale of the data.

- **Formula:**

$$\text{Normalized value} = \frac{X - \text{min}(X)}{\text{max}(X) - \text{min}(X)}$$

- **Use Cases:**

- When features have different units or scales (e.g., height in cm and weight in kg).

- Preparing data for algorithms that are sensitive to scale, such as KNN or SVM.

Standardization:

Standardization, or **z-score normalization**, transforms data to have a mean of 0 and a standard deviation of 1. This is useful when your data has outliers or you're working with algorithms like **linear regression** and **logistic regression** that assume data is normally distributed.

- **Formula**:

$$Z = \frac{X - \mu}{\sigma}$$

Where μ is the mean and σ is the standard deviation of the feature.

- **Use Cases**:

  - When working with algorithms that assume normal distribution (e.g., linear regression, logistic regression).

    ○ When features have significantly different ranges and need to be standardized for comparison.

Actionable Tips: Getting the Most Out of EDA

EDA is as much an art as it is a science, and knowing when and how to apply different techniques can make all the difference in uncovering hidden insights.

Quick Ways to Spot Outliers:

1. **Box Plots**: Outliers are easy to spot in box plots, as they appear as points outside the "whiskers" (the top and bottom ends of the box).

2. **Histograms**: Extreme values that fall far from the peak of the distribution are often outliers.

3. **Scatter Plots**: Outliers often appear as isolated points far from the cloud of other data points.

Choosing the Right Visualization for Different Data Types:

1. **Categorical Data:**

- o Use **bar charts** to show the frequency of each category.

- o **Pie charts** can be useful for displaying relative proportions of categories, but bar charts are generally more effective.

2. **Numerical Data:**

- o **Histograms** to show the distribution of a single feature.

- o **Box plots** to visualize the spread and detect outliers.

- o **Scatter plots** to explore relationships between two numerical variables.

3. **Multiple Variables:**

- o Use **pair plots** to visualize relationships between multiple numerical variables.

- o **Heatmaps** for correlation matrices to show the relationships between features in a compact form.

Hands-On Project: Visualizing Housing Prices

Now that you understand the key concepts in EDA, let's put them into practice with a **hands-on project**. In this example, we'll use **matplotlib** to create basic visualizations of a real-world dataset—**housing prices**.

Step 1: Load the Dataset:

We'll start by loading a real estate dataset containing information about house prices, square footage, and other features.

python

```python
import pandas as pd


# Load the housing dataset
data = pd.read_csv("housing_prices.csv")


# Display the first 5 rows
data.head()
```

Step 2: Visualize the Distribution of Prices:

We'll create a **histogram** to understand the distribution of house prices.

python

import matplotlib.pyplot as plt

 # Plot histogram of house prices

plt.hist(data['Price'], bins=30, edgecolor='black')

plt.title("Distribution of House Prices")

plt.xlabel("Price")

plt.ylabel("Frequency")

plt.show()

Step 3: Check for Outliers Using a Box Plot:

Next, let's use a **box plot** to check for any outliers in the prices.

python

 # Box plot of house prices

```
plt.boxplot(data['Price'])

plt.title("Box Plot of House Prices")

plt.ylabel("Price")

plt.show()
```

Step 4: Investigate the Relationship Between Size and Price:

Let's create a **scatter plot** to visualize the relationship between house size (square footage) and price.

python

```
# Scatter plot of square footage vs. price

plt.scatter(data['Square_Feet'], data['Price'])

plt.title("Square Footage vs Price")

plt.xlabel("Square Footage")

plt.ylabel("Price")

plt.show()
```

Step 5: Correlation Matrix:

Let's calculate the correlation between all numerical features and visualize it using a heatmap.

```python
import seaborn as sns

# Compute the correlation matrix
corr_matrix = data.corr()

# Plot heatmap of correlation matrix
sns.heatmap(corr_matrix, annot=True, cmap="coolwarm", linewidths=0.5)
plt.title("Correlation Matrix")
plt.show()
```

Conclusion

In this chapter, we've explored the essentials of **Exploratory Data Analysis (EDA)**—the first critical step in any machine learning project. By mastering data visualization techniques like histograms, box plots, scatter plots, and pair plots, you now have the tools to uncover hidden patterns and correlations in your data. Understanding the relationships between variables, as well as identifying outliers and data transformations, is crucial to building strong machine learning models.

Through the hands-on project, you've learned how to visualize and interpret a housing prices dataset, uncovering key insights such as price distributions, correlations between house size and price, and potential outliers.

As you continue your journey in machine learning, always remember that EDA is an iterative process. The deeper you go, the more insights you uncover, and the better equipped you'll be to build models that make accurate predictions.

Chapter 5: Machine Learning Fundamentals Without the Math Overload

Introduction

Machine learning (ML) is often viewed as a complex field filled with intimidating mathematical concepts. But the truth is, you don't need a Ph.D. in mathematics to understand and apply machine learning. In fact, one of the most effective ways to grasp machine learning is to focus on the **concepts** and **intuitions** behind the algorithms, without diving too deeply into the math.

In this chapter, we'll break down the core **machine learning paradigms** and introduce the fundamental ideas behind model training, model inference, and the balance between **overfitting** and **underfitting**. We'll also explore real-world analogies that make complex topics much easier to understand.

By the end of this chapter, you'll gain a strong conceptual understanding of machine learning, setting a solid foundation to build practical models. You'll also complete a hands-on project where we will implement a simple linear regression model to predict housing prices—focusing on the core idea of fitting a line to data, not the heavy math behind it.

Core Machine Learning Paradigms

Machine learning is a vast field with numerous approaches to solving different types of problems. However, most machine learning algorithms fall into one of three main paradigms:

1. **Supervised Learning**

2. **Unsupervised Learning**

3. **Reinforcement Learning**

Let's break down these paradigms, focusing on **intuitive** descriptions and **real-world analogies** to make the concepts more relatable.

---

1. Supervised Learning

Supervised learning is the most widely used form of machine learning. It's like having a **teacher** guide the model through the learning process. In supervised learning, the model is provided with **labeled data**—that is, data where the correct answer (label) is already known. The model's goal is to learn the relationship between the input (features) and the output (label), so it can predict the correct label for new, unseen data.

Real-World Analogy:

Imagine you're learning to recognize different types of fruit. You are shown pictures of various fruits (e.g., apple, banana, orange), and each picture comes with the correct label: **apple, banana, orange.** As you are shown more and more examples, you begin to associate certain features (e.g., color, shape, size) with each fruit. The more data you see, the better you get at recognizing new, unlabeled fruit that you haven't seen before.

In supervised learning, the **labeled data** serves as the teacher, guiding the model through the learning process. The model uses this information to **predict labels** for future data points.

- **Example**: Predicting house prices based on features like square footage, number of bedrooms, etc., where the actual price is provided in the training data. The model learns the relationship between features and the target price, enabling it to predict future prices.

Types of Supervised Learning:

- **Classification**: The goal is to assign data to one of several predefined categories. For example, classifying emails as "spam" or "not spam" is a classification problem.

- **Regression**: The goal is to predict a continuous numerical value. For example, predicting a house's price based on its features is a regression problem.

2. Unsupervised Learning

Unsupervised learning is a different approach where the model is given **unlabeled data**. There is no "teacher" guiding the process, and the model must figure out patterns and structures within the data on its own. The model tries to find hidden relationships, groupings, or patterns without any explicit guidance.

Real-World Analogy:

Think about a group of fruits being placed in front of you, but this time, **you don't know the labels**. Instead, you start noticing similarities: some fruits are round and red, others are long and yellow, and some are orange. Over time, you group the fruits based on these visual features. This is how **unsupervised learning** works—the model identifies similarities and clusters the data based on features.

- **Example**: A popular unsupervised learning task is **clustering**, such as grouping customers based on purchasing behavior or segmenting images based on color.

Types of Unsupervised Learning:

- **Clustering**: Grouping data into clusters where items in the same cluster are more similar to each other than to items in other clusters. K-means is a common clustering algorithm.

- **Dimensionality Reduction**: Reducing the number of features in the data while retaining important information. Techniques like **PCA (Principal Component Analysis)** fall under this category.

---

3. Reinforcement Learning

Reinforcement learning is a more advanced paradigm inspired by the way humans and animals learn. In reinforcement learning, the model learns by interacting with an environment and receiving feedback in the form of **rewards** or **penalties**. The model's goal is to maximize the cumulative reward over time by taking the most beneficial actions.

Real-World Analogy:

Imagine you're training a dog to fetch a ball. The dog tries different actions (e.g., running, sniffing, jumping) and receives rewards when it performs the correct action (e.g., bringing the ball back). Over time, the dog learns which actions lead to the most rewards and adjusts its behavior accordingly. In reinforcement learning, the **dog** is the model, and the **environment** is the world in which it learns.

- **Example**: A famous example of reinforcement learning is training a robot to play a video game. The robot receives rewards (points) based on its performance and adjusts its actions to maximize its score.

Model Training and Inference

Now that we've explored the core paradigms of machine learning, it's time to dive deeper into the process of **model training** and **model inference**. These are the two fundamental steps that occur in any machine learning workflow, regardless of the paradigm.

1. Model Training

Training a model is the process of teaching the model to learn patterns in the data. This is where the model gets its "knowledge" from the **labeled data** (in supervised learning) or the **unlabeled data** (in unsupervised learning). During training, the model **adjusts** its internal parameters to minimize the error between its predictions and the actual results. Essentially, the model "learns" by comparing its predictions to the true labels and adjusting its parameters to improve future predictions.

Real-World Analogy:

Let's go back to the fruit analogy. During training, you are shown pictures of fruits (with labels) repeatedly. Each time you make an error in identifying a fruit, you **correct your mistake** by adjusting your internal understanding of what makes an apple, banana, or orange. As you see more and more examples, your model (your ability to identify fruits) becomes more accurate.

- **In Supervised Learning**: The model uses the input features (e.g., square footage, number of bedrooms) and the corresponding target labels (e.g., house prices) to adjust its parameters.

- **In Unsupervised Learning**: The model uses input features alone to find patterns, such as clustering similar data points together.

2. Model Inference

After a model has been trained, the next step is **inference**. Inference is the process of using the trained model to make predictions on new, unseen data. In other words, you take the model you trained and use it to **infer** the outputs based on the input features of new examples.

Real-World Analogy:

Imagine you've trained a fruit-recognition model. Now, when you encounter a new fruit (an unseen example), you apply your trained model to predict whether it's an apple, banana, or orange. The model infers the label based on what it has learned from the training data.

- **In Supervised Learning**: After the model has learned the relationship between features and labels, it can predict the price of a house based on its size, number of rooms, etc.

- **In Unsupervised Learning**: After clustering data, the model can infer which group a new data point belongs to.

Overfitting vs. Underfitting

One of the most important concepts in machine learning is the balance between **overfitting** and **underfitting**. These two terms describe how well your model generalizes to new, unseen data.

Overfitting:

Overfitting occurs when a model **learns too much** from the training data, including noise, outliers, and irrelevant details. An overfitted model is too specific to the training data and may perform poorly on new data because it's essentially "memorized" the training data rather than learning general patterns.

Real-World Analogy:

Imagine you're trying to learn how to identify fruits, but instead of focusing on general characteristics (like color or shape), you memorize **every single detail** of the training fruits, such as their exact position in the image. When you encounter a new fruit in a different position, you'll fail to recognize it. Overfitting is like **memorizing** instead of learning.

- **Solution**: To prevent overfitting, use techniques like cross-validation, regularization, or pruning, and ensure you have enough diverse data.

Underfitting:

Underfitting occurs when a model is too **simple** and cannot capture the underlying patterns in the data. It fails to learn enough from the training data and, as a result, performs poorly on both the training and test sets.

Real-World Analogy:

Imagine you're trying to identify fruits, but you only know two things: fruit color and size. You can't recognize a fruit as well if you only focus on these simple features, missing out on other important characteristics like shape or texture. Underfitting is like **not learning enough** to make accurate predictions.

- **Solution**: To prevent underfitting, use more complex models or more relevant features in your data.

Balancing Overfitting and Underfitting:

The key to successful machine learning is finding the **sweet spot** between overfitting and underfitting. You want your model to generalize well to new data while still capturing the underlying patterns of the training data. This balance can be achieved through:

- Proper data preprocessing.

- Choosing the right model complexity.

- Using techniques like **regularization** and **cross-validation**.

Hands-On Project: Implementing Linear Regression to Predict House Prices

Now that we've built a strong understanding of machine learning fundamentals, let's implement a **simple linear regression** model to predict house prices. We'll focus on the **conceptual understanding** of fitting a line to data, not the complex mathematics behind it.

Step 1: Load the Dataset

We'll use the **housing dataset**, which contains features like **square footage** and **price**.

python

import pandas as pd

```
# Load the housing dataset

data = pd.read_csv("housing_prices.csv")


# Display the first few rows

data.head()
```

Step 2: Visualize the Data

Let's create a scatter plot to see the relationship between house size and price.

python

```
import matplotlib.pyplot as plt


# Scatter plot of square footage vs. price

plt.scatter(data['Square_Feet'], data['Price'])

plt.title("Square Footage vs Price")

plt.xlabel("Square Footage")

plt.ylabel("Price")

plt.show()
```

Step 3: Train the Model

We'll use the **scikit-learn** library to implement a simple linear regression model. First, we'll separate our data into input features and target labels.

python

```
from sklearn.linear_model import LinearRegression

# Select the feature and target
X = data[['Square_Feet']]  # Input feature (square footage)
y = data['Price']       # Target label (price)

# Initialize the model
model = LinearRegression()

# Train the model
model.fit(X, y)
```

Step 4: Make Predictions

Now that the model is trained, we can use it to make predictions.

python

```
# Predict house prices for the same input data

predictions = model.predict(X)


# Plot the original data and the predicted line

plt.scatter(data['Square_Feet'], data['Price'], color='blue')

plt.plot(data['Square_Feet'], predictions, color='red',
linewidth=2)

plt.title("Linear Regression: Square Footage vs Price")

plt.xlabel("Square Footage")

plt.ylabel("Price")

plt.show()
```

Step 5: Evaluate the Model

To evaluate the performance of our model, we can use metrics like **Mean Squared Error (MSE).**

python

from sklearn.metrics import mean_squared_error

 # Calculate the Mean Squared Error

mse = mean_squared_error(y, predictions)

print(f"Mean Squared Error: {mse}")

Conclusion

In this chapter, we explored the fundamental paradigms of machine learning—supervised learning, unsupervised learning, and reinforcement learning—while also breaking down the concepts of **model training** and **model inference**. We tackled the issue of **overfitting vs. underfitting** and provided analogies that simplify these core ideas.

By implementing a **linear regression model**, we saw how a machine learning algorithm can be used to **predict** house prices based on their size. Through this hands-on project, you gained valuable experience in understanding the core concepts of machine learning without getting bogged down in complex math.

With these conceptual building blocks in place, you're ready to dive deeper into more advanced machine learning algorithms and continue experimenting with real-world data. The most important takeaway? Machine learning is about **understanding the concepts and patterns** that the algorithms reveal—everything else will fall into place as you gain more experience.

Chapter 6: Introduction to Predictive Modeling (Classification & Regression)

Introduction

In the world of machine learning, **predictive modeling** is the art of creating models that can forecast future events based on data. Predictive modeling involves using historical data to build models that can predict future outcomes, and it is fundamental to solving a wide array of problems across various industries. Whether you're trying to predict customer churn, classify emails as spam or not, or forecast housing prices, predictive modeling is key.

In this chapter, we will dive into two of the most common types of predictive modeling: **classification** and **regression**. We'll cover the foundational concepts behind popular algorithms like **Logistic Regression**, **Decision Trees**, and **Linear Regression**, and we'll explain the performance metrics used to evaluate the models.

By the end of this chapter, you'll have a solid understanding of these algorithms and the ability to apply them in real-world scenarios, such as classifying emails or predicting car prices.

What is Predictive Modeling?

Predictive modeling involves using data and statistical algorithms to identify the likelihood of future outcomes. It is used in various industries to make informed decisions, improve operational efficiency, and gain deeper insights into consumer behavior.

Predictive models are usually built on **historical data** and then used to predict **future outcomes**. These models help businesses and organizations anticipate future trends and make data-driven decisions.

There are two primary types of predictive modeling tasks:

- **Classification**: When the output is a category or label (e.g., spam or not spam).

- **Regression**: When the output is a continuous numerical value (e.g., price prediction or sales forecast).

Classification Models

In classification tasks, the goal is to predict which category or class an observation belongs to based on its features. For example, classifying emails as spam or not spam, or determining whether a tumor is malignant or benign. These tasks have discrete, categorical outcomes.

1. Logistic Regression

Despite its name, **Logistic Regression** is a classification algorithm, not a regression algorithm. It is used to predict binary outcomes—two classes. Logistic Regression models the probability that an observation belongs to a particular class.

How It Works:

Logistic Regression applies the **logistic function (sigmoid function)** to the linear combination of input features to produce an output probability. This probability is then thresholded to assign the observation to one of two classes.

- **Equation:**

  $P(y=1|x) = \frac{1}{1 + e^{-(w_0 + w_1x_1 + w_2x_2 + \ldots + w_nx_n)}}$ Where:

  - $P(y=1|x)$ is the probability of the observation belonging to class 1.

  - $w_0, w_1, \ldots, w_n$ are the coefficients of the model.

  - $x_1, x_2, \ldots, x_n$ are the input features.

Logistic regression uses the **logit function** to map continuous input data to probabilities. Once the probability is calculated, a **threshold** is applied to decide the class.

Real-World Example:

In a **spam email classification** task, Logistic Regression could predict whether an email is spam or not based on features like the presence of certain words, sender information, and more.

2. Decision Trees for Classification

A **Decision Tree** is a tree-like model used for both classification and regression tasks. It splits the data into branches based on feature values and makes predictions by following these branches down to the leaves, where each leaf represents a class label.

How It Works:

A Decision Tree recursively splits the data into subsets based on the feature that results in the largest **information gain** (or **Gini impurity reduction**). This process is repeated at each internal node until the data points within each subset belong to the same class, or until a stopping condition is reached.

The model makes a prediction by following the decisions at each node and ending up at a leaf node, which assigns a label to the observation.

- **Real-World Example**: A **Decision Tree** could classify emails based on the frequency of certain words. For example, if the email contains the word "free," it might be classified as spam.

Regression Models

Regression models are used when the output is a continuous value. Unlike classification, which has discrete categories, regression predicts numerical outcomes. For instance, predicting housing prices based on features like square footage, number of bedrooms, etc., is a regression task.

1. Linear Regression

Linear Regression is one of the simplest and most widely used regression models. It predicts the relationship between a dependent variable (target) and one or more independent variables (features) by fitting a linear equation to the observed data.

How It Works:

Linear Regression models the relationship between the target variable y and the input features $x_1, x_2, \ldots, x_n$ using a linear equation:

$$y = w_0 + w_1 x_1 + w_2 x_2 + \ldots + w_n x_n + \epsilon$$

Where:

- y is the predicted value.
- $w_0, w_1, \ldots, w_n$ are the coefficients (weights) of the model.
- $x_1, x_2, \ldots, x_n$ are the features.
- ϵ is the error term.

The goal of Linear Regression is to find the values of $w_0, w_1, \ldots, w_n$ that minimize the **mean squared error (MSE)** between the predicted and actual values.

Real-World Example:

In a **car price prediction** task, Linear Regression can predict the price of a car based on features like age, mileage, brand, and model. The model would fit a line that best describes the relationship between these features and the price.

2. Decision Trees for Regression

Decision Trees for Regression work similarly to classification Decision Trees but instead of predicting class labels, they predict continuous values. The tree splits the data based on the feature that reduces the error (usually **mean squared error**), and predictions are made by averaging the values of the observations in each leaf node.

How It Works:

The Decision Tree algorithm for regression recursively splits the data based on features that result in the best reduction in error. The target prediction for each leaf node is the **mean value** of the observations in that leaf.

Real-World Example:

Predicting **house prices** using a Decision Tree might involve splitting the data based on features like square footage, number of bedrooms, and neighborhood. The tree will make predictions based on the average house price in the corresponding leaf.

Performance Metrics

Evaluating the performance of a machine learning model is crucial to understanding how well it will perform on unseen data. Several performance metrics are used, depending on whether the task is classification or regression.

1. Classification Performance Metrics

Accuracy:

Accuracy is the percentage of correct predictions made by the model. It is the most straightforward metric for classification models but can be misleading when the dataset is imbalanced (e.g., when one class is much more frequent than the other).

$$\text{Accuracy} = \frac{\text{Correct Predictions}}{\text{Total Predictions}}$$

Precision:

Precision measures the proportion of positive predictions that are actually correct. It is useful when the cost of false positives is high (e.g., predicting a non-spam email as spam).

$$\text{Precision} = \frac{\text{True Positives}}{\text{True Positives + False Positives}}$$

Recall (Sensitivity):

Recall measures the proportion of actual positive instances that are correctly identified. It is important when the cost of false negatives is high (e.g., not detecting a fraudulent transaction).

$$\text{Recall} = \frac{\text{True Positives}}{\text{True Positives + False}}$$

Negatives}}Recall=True Positives + False NegativesTru e Positives

F1-Score:

The **F1-score** is the harmonic mean of precision and recall. It provides a balanced view of a model's performance, especially when the class distribution is imbalanced.

F1-Score=2×Precision×RecallPrecision + Recall\text{F1-Score} = \frac{2 \times \text{Precision} \times \text{Recall}}{\text{Precision + Recall}}F1-Score=Precision + Recall2×Precision×Recall

Confusion Matrix:

A **confusion matrix** is a table that is often used to evaluate classification models. It shows the number of true positives, true negatives, false positives, and false negatives. From this matrix, you can calculate other performance metrics like accuracy, precision, recall, and F1-score.

2. Regression Performance Metrics

Mean Squared Error (MSE):

MSE measures the average squared difference between predicted and actual values. It's one of the most common performance metrics for regression.

$$\text{MSE} = \frac{1}{n} \sum_{i=1}^{n} (y_i - \hat{y_i})^2$$

Where:

- y_i is the true value.

- $\hat{y_i}$ is the predicted value.

Root Mean Squared Error (RMSE):

RMSE is the square root of MSE and gives an idea of the magnitude of the error in the original units of the target variable.

$$\text{RMSE} = \sqrt{\text{MSE}}$$

RMSE is useful for understanding how far off your model's predictions are on average, with a lower RMSE indicating better performance.

Real-World Applications

Let's explore some **real-world applications** where classification and regression are used to make predictions.

1. Email Spam Classification

Spam filters use classification models to predict whether an email is spam or not. Features like the sender's email, subject line, frequency of certain keywords, and the presence of attachments help the model classify the email into either the **spam** or **non-spam** category.

2. Predicting Car Prices

Predicting the price of a car is a regression task. Features like the car's **age, mileage, make, model,** and **condition** can be used to predict its price. Linear regression or decision trees for regression are often used in this type of prediction.

3. Insurance Costs Prediction

Insurance companies use regression models to predict the cost of premiums for different customers based on features like **age, driving history**, and **location**.

4. Customer Churn Prediction

Classification models are used by businesses to predict customer churn—whether or not a customer will leave. Features such as **purchase history, customer service interactions,** and **subscription length** can help predict the likelihood of churn.

Hands-On Project: Building a Decision Tree Classifier

Now that we've discussed classification and regression, let's build a simple classification model using a **Decision Tree**. We'll use a small dataset, such as the **Iris dataset**, which contains features about flowers and their species.

Step 1: Load the Dataset

python

```
import pandas as pd

from sklearn.datasets import load_iris


# Load the Iris dataset
```

```python
data = load_iris()

X = data.data

y = data.target


# Convert to DataFrame for easier handling

df = pd.DataFrame(X, columns=data.feature_names)

df['species'] = y

df.head()
```

Step 2: Split the Data

Before training the model, we'll split the data into training and testing sets to evaluate its performance.

python

```python
from sklearn.model_selection import train_test_split


# Split the data into training and testing sets

X_train, X_test, y_train, y_test = train_test_split(X, y, test_size=0.3, random_state=42)
```

Step 3: Train the Decision Tree Classifier

python

```
from sklearn.tree import DecisionTreeClassifier

# Initialize the classifier
clf = DecisionTreeClassifier()

# Train the model
clf.fit(X_train, y_train)
```

Step 4: Evaluate the Model Using Accuracy and Confusion Matrix

python

```
from sklearn.metrics import accuracy_score, confusion_matrix

# Make predictions on the test data
y_pred = clf.predict(X_test)
```

```python
# Calculate accuracy

accuracy = accuracy_score(y_test, y_pred)

print(f"Accuracy: {accuracy}")
```

```python
# Generate confusion matrix

conf_matrix = confusion_matrix(y_test, y_pred)

print("Confusion Matrix:")

print(conf_matrix)
```

Step 5: Visualize the Decision Tree

python

```python
from sklearn.tree import plot_tree
```

```python
# Plot the decision tree

plt.figure(figsize=(12, 8))

plot_tree(clf, filled=True, feature_names=data.feature_names,
class_names=data.target_names)
```

plt.show()

Conclusion

In this chapter, we covered the essentials of **predictive modeling**—focusing on classification and regression tasks. We discussed important algorithms like **Logistic Regression, Decision Trees**, and **Linear Regression**, and explored real-world applications such as spam classification and price prediction.

We also introduced **performance metrics** for both classification and regression, helping you evaluate the performance of your models in a meaningful way.

Finally, we put theory into practice by building a **Decision Tree Classifier** to predict flower species from the Iris dataset. This hands-on project reinforced your understanding of classification and model evaluation.

By understanding these foundational concepts and algorithms, you're now ready to tackle more complex predictive modeling tasks and apply machine learning techniques to real-world problems.

Chapter 7: Feature Engineering & Model Improvement

Introduction

In machine learning, the data you feed to your model is paramount. While algorithms like Decision Trees, Linear Regression, and Neural Networks are the driving force behind predictions, the **quality of the data** determines how effectively these algorithms perform. Enter **feature engineering**: the process of transforming raw data into a form that is more suitable for machine learning models.

Feature engineering can make or break your model. In fact, many successful machine learning practitioners spend a significant amount of time on feature engineering to improve the performance of their models, often more than tuning the model itself. With well-engineered features, even simple models can outperform more complex ones.

This chapter will cover the basics of **feature engineering** and **model improvement**. We'll dive into strategies like **one-hot encoding, feature scaling,** and **polynomial features.** We'll also explore **hyperparameter tuning** techniques like **grid search** and **random search,** providing you with the tools to fine-tune your models for optimal performance.

By the end of this chapter, you'll understand how to manipulate your data and model to get the best possible results, and you'll be equipped to take on more advanced machine learning projects.

What is Feature Engineering, and Why is it Crucial?

Feature engineering is the process of creating new input features or modifying existing ones to improve the performance of a machine learning model. It involves transforming raw data into meaningful features that highlight important patterns and relationships in the data.

Good feature engineering can:

- **Boost model accuracy**: By providing the algorithm with more relevant or informative data, feature engineering can lead to better predictions.

- **Reduce model complexity**: Properly engineered features can make simpler models more effective, reducing the need for complex algorithms or large amounts of data.

- **Speed up learning**: Clean, well-engineered features can help the model learn faster and converge to optimal solutions more quickly.

While a machine learning algorithm can learn on its own, its performance heavily depends on the data it's trained on. If the features provided aren't insightful or relevant, even the most sophisticated model won't perform well.

Why Feature Engineering Matters:

Imagine you're trying to predict house prices based on features like square footage and number of bedrooms. If your dataset also includes neighborhood information, such as proximity to schools or crime rates, these additional features could greatly improve the model's ability to predict prices accurately.

In contrast, if your dataset includes irrelevant features—like a column indicating the color of the house—this could introduce noise and reduce the model's performance. Feature engineering helps ensure that the algorithm only learns from the most informative features.

Strategies for Feature Engineering

There are several common strategies for feature engineering that can dramatically improve model performance. Let's break them down.

1. One-Hot Encoding

One-hot encoding is a technique used to convert categorical features into a numerical format that machine learning models can work with. Many models require numerical input, and **one-hot**

encoding creates binary (0 or 1) columns for each category within a categorical feature.

Why It's Needed:

Most machine learning algorithms, such as Linear Regression or Decision Trees, can't process categorical variables directly (like "red", "blue", "green"). These variables must be transformed into a numerical format to be useful.

How It Works:

One-hot encoding turns a categorical feature into multiple binary features, each representing one of the possible categories. For example, a "Color" column with three categories: "red", "blue", and "green", would be transformed into three columns: "Color_red", "Color_blue", and "Color_green". If the original row had a color of "blue", the transformed values would be: [0, 1, 0].

Real-World Example:

If you're working with an email spam detection system, one of the categorical features might be the **sender's email domain** ("gmail.com", "yahoo.com", "outlook.com"). One-hot encoding would transform this feature into three binary features, each representing one of the email domains.

Example in Code:

python

import pandas as pd

 # Sample dataset with a categorical feature

data = pd.DataFrame({'Color': ['red', 'blue', 'green', 'blue', 'red']})

 # Apply one-hot encoding

data_encoded = pd.get_dummies(data, columns=['Color'])

print(data_encoded)

This would output:

nginx

	red	blue	green
0	1	0	0
1	0	1	0
2	0	0	1
3	0	1	0
4	1	0	0

2. Feature Scaling

Many machine learning algorithms, like **K-Nearest Neighbors (KNN)** and **Support Vector Machines (SVM)**, are sensitive to the scale of the data. **Feature scaling** ensures that all features contribute equally to the model by transforming them into a standard range.

Types of Scaling:

- **Normalization (Min-Max Scaling)**: Rescales the data into a range between 0 and 1. The formula for normalization is:

Xscaled=X−XminXmax−XminX_{\text{scaled}} = \frac{X - X_{\text{min}}}{X_{\text{max}} - X_{\text{min}}}Xscaled =Xmax−XminX−Xmin

- **Standardization (Z-Score Normalization):** Scales the data to have a mean of 0 and a standard deviation of 1. The formula for standardization is:

$Z=X-μσZ = \frac{X - \mu}{\sigma}Z=σX−μ$

Where μ\muµ is the mean and σ\sigmaσ is the standard deviation of the feature.

Why It's Important:

Without scaling, features with larger ranges (e.g., income in the range of 1000-100,000) will dominate features with smaller ranges (e.g., age in the range of 20-70). Scaling ensures that the model treats all features equally.

Example in Code:

python

from sklearn.preprocessing import StandardScaler

 # Sample dataset

data = pd.DataFrame({'Age': [25, 30, 35, 40, 45], 'Income': [50000, 60000, 70000, 80000, 90000]})

```
# Apply Standardization

scaler = StandardScaler()

data_scaled = scaler.fit_transform(data)


# Convert back to a DataFrame

data_scaled_df = pd.DataFrame(data_scaled, columns=['Age',
'Income'])

print(data_scaled_df)
```

---

3. Polynomial Features

Sometimes, the relationship between features and the target variable is not linear. **Polynomial features** allow you to create new features by raising existing features to higher powers. This can help capture non-linear relationships between the data and improve model accuracy.

Why It's Useful:

Polynomial features introduce new, higher-order relationships between features. For instance, if you believe the relationship between square footage and house price is quadratic, polynomial features could help capture that non-linear relationship.

How It Works:

If you have a feature xxx, polynomial features would create additional features such as $x2x^2x2$, $x3x^3x3$, etc. These features allow the model to fit non-linear curves instead of just straight lines.

Example in Code:

python

```
from sklearn.preprocessing import PolynomialFeatures

# Sample dataset
data = pd.DataFrame({'Square_Feet': [1000, 1500, 2000, 2500, 3000]})

# Apply Polynomial Features
poly = PolynomialFeatures(degree=2)  # Generates x^2 and the original feature x
```

```
data_poly = poly.fit_transform(data)


# Convert back to a DataFrame

data_poly_df = pd.DataFrame(data_poly, columns=['Intercept',
'Square_Feet', 'Square_Feet^2'])

print(data_poly_df)
```

Hyperparameter Tuning: Grid Search & Random Search

Once you've engineered your features, you can improve your model's performance by tuning its **hyperparameters**. Hyperparameters are the settings that control how the machine learning algorithm works. For example, in a decision tree, hyperparameters might include the **maximum depth** of the tree or the **minimum samples per leaf**.

Tuning hyperparameters helps find the combination of settings that gives the best model performance.

1. Grid Search

Grid Search is a brute-force approach to hyperparameter tuning. It exhaustively searches through all possible combinations of a predefined set of hyperparameters. For each combination, it trains and evaluates the model, eventually selecting the best combination based on performance metrics.

How It Works:

1. You define a grid of possible hyperparameter values.

2. Grid search trains the model with every combination of values in the grid.

3. The best combination is selected based on evaluation metrics like accuracy or mean squared error.

2. Random Search

Random Search is a more efficient method of hyperparameter tuning. Instead of searching through all possible combinations, random search randomly selects a subset of hyperparameters from the grid. While it might not explore all possibilities, it can often find good solutions with fewer trials.

Example in Code:

python

```python
from sklearn.model_selection import GridSearchCV


# Sample decision tree classifier
from sklearn.tree import DecisionTreeClassifier


# Define the parameter grid
param_grid = {'max_depth': [5, 10, 15, 20], 'min_samples_split':
[2, 5, 10]}


# Initialize the classifier
clf = DecisionTreeClassifier()


# Apply Grid Search
grid_search = GridSearchCV(clf, param_grid, cv=5)
grid_search.fit(X_train, y_train)


# Get the best parameters
print("Best parameters:", grid_search.best_params_)
```

Real-World Example: Transforming Raw Text Data for Spam Detection

Text data is inherently unstructured, and before it can be used in machine learning models, it must be transformed into a usable form. **Text vectorization** is a form of feature engineering that converts text into numerical representations.

1. Bag-of-Words:

The **Bag-of-Words** model is one of the simplest text vectorization techniques. It transforms each word in the document into a unique feature, creating a large, sparse matrix.

2. TF-IDF (Term Frequency-Inverse Document Frequency):

TF-IDF is a more sophisticated technique that weights each word by how important it is to a document in relation to a collection of documents. Words that appear frequently in a document but rarely in other documents are given more importance.

Example:

To transform raw text data into features, we can use libraries like **CountVectorizer** or **TfidfVectorizer** from **scikit-learn**.

python

```python
from sklearn.feature_extraction.text import TfidfVectorizer

# Sample text data
text_data = ['Free money now!', 'Important message from your bank.', 'Congratulations, you won a prize!']

# Apply TF-IDF vectorization
vectorizer = TfidfVectorizer()
X = vectorizer.fit_transform(text_data)

print(X.toarray())  # The transformed feature matrix
```

Hands-On Project: Feature Engineering & Model Improvement

Now that we've covered the theoretical aspects, let's put it into practice. We will start with a basic classification model and improve it step by step by adding new features or tuning hyperparameters.

Step 1: Start with a Basic Model

Let's begin with a simple Decision Tree classifier to predict whether an email is spam based on its content. We will use the **SMS Spam Collection** dataset, which contains labeled examples of spam and ham (non-spam) messages.

Step 2: Apply One-Hot Encoding

First, we will encode the target variable (spam vs. ham) into binary values (1 for spam, 0 for ham).

python

```
# Sample data
data = pd.DataFrame({
    'message': ['Free money now!', 'Important message from your
bank.', 'Congratulations, you won a prize!'],
```

'label': ['spam', 'ham', 'spam']

})

 # Apply one-hot encoding

data['label'] = data['label'].map({'spam': 1, 'ham': 0})

 # Now the target variable is binary

print(data)

Step 3: Feature Scaling

Before applying any algorithms, it's a good practice to scale numerical features. Since our dataset is text-based, we will focus on scaling after vectorization.

Step 4: Apply Hyperparameter Tuning

Now, let's improve the model by tuning hyperparameters using **Random Search**.

python

from sklearn.model_selection import RandomizedSearchCV

from sklearn.tree import DecisionTreeClassifier

```
# Set up the classifier and hyperparameters
clf = DecisionTreeClassifier()


param_dist = {
    'max_depth': [5, 10, 15, 20],
    'min_samples_split': [2, 5, 10],
}


# Apply Randomized Search
random_search = RandomizedSearchCV(clf, param_dist, cv=5)
random_search.fit(X_train, y_train)


# Best parameters
print("Best Parameters:", random_search.best_params_)
```

Step 5: Evaluate the Model

Finally, we will evaluate the model's performance using the **confusion matrix** and **accuracy score**.

python

```
from sklearn.metrics import accuracy_score, confusion_matrix

# Make predictions on the test set
y_pred = random_search.predict(X_test)

# Evaluate the model
accuracy = accuracy_score(y_test, y_pred)
print(f"Accuracy: {accuracy}")
print(f"Confusion Matrix:\n{confusion_matrix(y_test, y_pred)}")
```

Conclusion

Feature engineering and model improvement are essential skills for any machine learning practitioner. By understanding how to **transform raw data into**

informative features, you can significantly boost the performance of your models. Techniques like **one-hot encoding, feature scaling**, and **polynomial features** are all tools in your arsenal for improving model accuracy.

Equally important is **hyperparameter tuning**. By fine-tuning your model's parameters through techniques like **grid search** and **random search**, you ensure that your model is running optimally.

Through this chapter's hands-on project, you've seen firsthand how feature engineering and hyperparameter tuning can be applied to a classification task. As you continue working on machine learning projects, remember that feature engineering is often the key to unlocking better performance and more accurate predictions.

Chapter 8: Ensemble Methods & Advanced Algorithms Made Simple

Introduction

In the world of machine learning, there's a powerful and often overlooked concept that significantly improves model accuracy and robustness—**ensemble methods**. While simple models like **Decision Trees** are widely used for their simplicity and interpretability, ensemble methods, which combine multiple individual models to produce a stronger model, often deliver superior results. These methods are essential in many real-world applications, ranging from recommendation systems to fraud detection.

In this chapter, we will explore **Random Forests** and **Gradient Boosted Trees**—two of the most widely used ensemble methods in machine learning. We'll break down why ensembles are so effective, how they work, and when you should choose ensemble methods over simpler models. We'll also cover the trade-offs involved, including the impact of ensemble methods on computational cost and model interpretability.

Finally, we'll walk through a hands-on project where you'll compare the performance of a **single Decision Tree** with that of a **Random Forest** on the same dataset. By the end of this chapter, you will not only understand ensemble methods but also gain practical experience in implementing them.

What Are Ensemble Methods?

At the core of ensemble methods is the idea of combining multiple models, often referred to as **weak**

learners, to create a stronger model, or **strong learner**. The basic premise is that by leveraging the **wisdom of the crowd**, you can build a model that is more accurate and less prone to errors than any single model in the ensemble.

Why Ensembles Often Outperform Single Models:

Ensemble methods work under the assumption that the combined prediction of several models will outperform the prediction of any single model. The key reasons for this are:

- **Reduction in overfitting**: Single models, especially complex ones, may overfit to the training data, capturing noise as if it were a signal. Ensembles tend to smooth out these noise effects.

- **Improved generalization**: When you average multiple models, their individual biases can cancel out, leading to better generalization to unseen data.

- **Robustness**: Ensembles are more robust because they are less sensitive to small changes in the data, making them more stable across different datasets.

While individual models might fail in specific areas, an ensemble can perform better because it combines the strengths of various models, which is particularly useful when dealing with noisy data or complex datasets.

Key Ensemble Methods

Now that we understand why ensembles work, let's explore two of the most widely used ensemble methods in machine learning: **Random Forests** and **Gradient Boosted Trees**.

1. Random Forests

A **Random Forest** is an ensemble method that combines many **Decision Trees** to create a powerful and robust model. The key idea behind Random Forests is to **randomly sample** the data and features for each tree in the forest, allowing the model to learn diverse patterns from the data.

How It Works:

Random Forests are built by creating multiple **Decision Trees**, each trained on a random subset of the data (via **bootstrap sampling**, meaning sampling with replacement). Each tree in the forest makes its own prediction, and the final prediction is determined by aggregating the predictions of all the trees:

- **For regression** tasks, the final prediction is the **average** of all tree predictions.

- **For classification** tasks, the final prediction is the **majority vote** across all trees.

Random Forests also introduce randomness in the feature selection process, where each tree is only allowed to split on a random subset of features at each node. This further reduces overfitting by making trees less correlated with one another.

Why Random Forests Are Powerful:

- **Reduced overfitting**: The randomness introduced through bootstrap sampling and feature selection makes Random Forests less likely to overfit compared to a single Decision Tree.

- **Handles both classification and regression**: Random Forests can be used for both classification and regression tasks.

- **Robust to outliers**: Random Forests are not sensitive to outliers, as the model aggregates predictions from many trees, making it more stable.

Real-World Example:

Random Forests have been used in a variety of real-world applications, such as:

- **Fraud detection**: In banking, Random Forests are used to identify fraudulent transactions based on patterns in spending behavior.

- **Customer churn prediction**: Companies like telecom providers use Random Forests to predict which customers are likely to leave by analyzing their usage patterns and demographic data.

2. Gradient Boosting Trees

Gradient Boosting is another powerful ensemble method that builds models sequentially, with each new model trying to correct the errors made by the previous models. Unlike Random Forests, which build trees independently, Gradient Boosting focuses on reducing errors by fitting new models to the residual errors of prior models.

How It Works:

- **Boosting** refers to the sequential nature of the method. Each new tree is trained to predict the residual errors (the difference between actual and predicted values) from the previous tree.

- The predictions of all trees are combined to give the final output. Typically, this is done through a weighted average or weighted sum.

- **Gradient Boosting** uses the gradient descent algorithm to minimize the loss function (such as mean squared error for regression or log loss for classification).

In Gradient Boosting, each new model is added to improve the performance of the ensemble by focusing on the errors made by previous models. This is done by **minimizing a loss function**, usually with respect to the **gradient** of the error.

Why Gradient Boosting Is Powerful:

- **High predictive accuracy**: Gradient Boosting tends to achieve very high accuracy, particularly in cases where the data is noisy and complex.

- **Handles imbalanced datasets well**: Gradient Boosting can be fine-tuned to work well with imbalanced data, where certain classes are underrepresented.

- **Customizable loss functions**: You can customize the loss function to suit the specific problem you're solving.

Real-World Example:

Gradient Boosting is widely used in high-performance predictive modeling. Some examples include:

- **Kaggle competitions**: Gradient Boosting is often the go-to algorithm for winning solutions in Kaggle competitions, such as those for predicting housing prices, sales forecasting, and customer behavior analysis.

- **Recommendation systems**: Companies like Amazon and Netflix use Gradient Boosting to predict what products or shows a user is likely to prefer based on historical preferences.

When to Use Ensemble Methods vs. Simpler Models

Ensemble methods like Random Forests and Gradient Boosted Trees are incredibly powerful, but they're not always the right choice. There are cases where simpler models might be more effective or more appropriate, depending on the nature of the problem and the constraints of the project.

When to Use Ensemble Methods:

- **When accuracy is paramount**: Ensemble methods often outperform individual models, especially when dealing with noisy, high-dimensional, or complex data.

- **When the dataset is large**: If you have a large dataset with many features, ensemble methods like Random Forests and Gradient Boosting can handle this complexity well.

- **When interpretability is less important**: Ensemble methods, especially Gradient Boosting, can be less interpretable than simpler models. If interpretability is not a top priority, these models can be a great choice.

When to Use Simpler Models:

- **When interpretability is key**: Simple models like Decision Trees and Linear Regression are more interpretable, which is crucial in domains where understanding the decision-making process is important (e.g., healthcare or finance).

- **When computational resources are limited**: Ensemble methods, especially Gradient Boosting, can be computationally expensive and require more memory. In such cases, simpler models may be a better choice.

- **When the dataset is small**: Ensemble methods tend to perform better with larger datasets. If the dataset is small, simpler models may be sufficient and will train faster.

Cautions About Computational Cost and Interpretability

While ensemble methods provide excellent predictive power, they come with trade-offs. Here are some key factors to consider:

Computational Cost:

- **Random Forests** and **Gradient Boosting** can be computationally expensive, especially when dealing with large datasets or many trees. Training these models may take more time and resources than simpler models.

- **Hyperparameter tuning** for ensemble methods (especially Gradient Boosting) can further increase computation time, as it requires searching over a range of hyperparameters, which can be computationally intensive.

Interpretability:

- Ensemble methods, especially **Gradient Boosting**, are often referred to as "black-box" models. This means that, while they provide high predictive accuracy, it can be difficult to explain why they make certain predictions.

- **Random Forests** are somewhat more interpretable than Gradient Boosting, as individual trees can be examined, but they are still less interpretable than a simple Decision Tree.

For applications where transparency is important (such as medical or financial decision-making), simpler models may be preferred.

Hands-On Project: Compare a Decision Tree vs. a Random Forest

Now, let's put these ensemble techniques into practice. We'll build a **Decision Tree** and a **Random Forest** to classify a dataset, then compare their performance.

Step 1: Load the Dataset

For this project, we'll use the **Iris dataset**, which contains information about different species of flowers based on features like sepal length, sepal width, petal length, and petal width.

python

import pandas as pd

from sklearn.datasets import load_iris

 # Load the Iris dataset

```python
data = load_iris()

X = data.data

y = data.target
```

Step 2: Train a Decision Tree Classifier

First, we'll train a single **Decision Tree** classifier on the dataset.

python

```python
from sklearn.tree import DecisionTreeClassifier

from sklearn.model_selection import train_test_split


# Split the data into training and testing sets

X_train, X_test, y_train, y_test = train_test_split(X, y, test_size=0.3, random_state=42)


# Train a Decision Tree

dt_model = DecisionTreeClassifier(random_state=42)

dt_model.fit(X_train, y_train)
```

Step 3: Train a Random Forest Classifier

Next, we'll train a **Random Forest** classifier on the same data.

python

```python
from sklearn.ensemble import RandomForestClassifier


# Train a Random Forest model
rf_model = RandomForestClassifier(random_state=42)
rf_model.fit(X_train, y_train)
```

Step 4: Evaluate the Models

Now we'll evaluate both models using **accuracy**.

python

```python
from sklearn.metrics import accuracy_score


# Predict with both models
dt_pred = dt_model.predict(X_test)
```

```
rf_pred = rf_model.predict(X_test)
```

```
# Calculate accuracy

dt_accuracy = accuracy_score(y_test, dt_pred)

rf_accuracy = accuracy_score(y_test, rf_pred)
```

```
print(f"Decision Tree Accuracy: {dt_accuracy}")

print(f"Random Forest Accuracy: {rf_accuracy}")
```

Step 5: Compare the Results

You should see that the **Random Forest** classifier performs better than the **Decision Tree**, demonstrating how ensemble methods often improve accuracy.

Conclusion

In this chapter, we explored the power of **ensemble methods** and why they often outperform individual models. We examined **Random Forests** and **Gradient Boosting**, two of the most powerful ensemble techniques, and discussed their real-world applications in areas like spam detection, fraud prevention, and recommendation systems.

We also covered important considerations such as **computational cost** and **model interpretability**, which are key trade-offs when deciding whether to use an ensemble method.

Finally, through a hands-on project, we compared the performance of a **Decision Tree** and a **Random Forest** on the Iris dataset, demonstrating how feature engineering and ensemble methods can lead to significant improvements in model accuracy.

Armed with this knowledge, you're now ready to use ensemble methods to tackle more complex machine learning problems and make smarter decisions about when to use these powerful techniques.

Chapter 9: Deep Learning Basics – Demystifying Neural Networks

Introduction

Deep learning has revolutionized the field of machine learning, powering some of the most impressive technological advancements of recent years. Whether it's **self-driving cars** navigating city streets, **voice assistants** transcribing your speech into text, or **image recognition** systems identifying objects in photos, deep learning is at the core of these innovations.

However, for many, the concept of **neural networks**—the foundation of deep learning—can seem intimidating. This chapter will demystify neural networks and provide a **simple, intuitive explanation** of how they work. We will introduce the basic building blocks of neural networks, explain the different types of networks, and explore how they are used in real-world applications.

We will also take a hands-on approach, building a basic **feedforward neural network** to classify handwritten digits from the **MNIST dataset**, all while keeping the explanations **math-free** and focused on understanding the concepts and processes behind neural networks.

By the end of this chapter, you'll have a clear understanding of how neural networks work and how to implement them using popular frameworks like **TensorFlow** and **PyTorch**. Let's dive in!

What is a Neural Network?

A **neural network** is a computational model inspired by the way biological brains work. Just as neurons in the brain work together to process information, artificial neurons (also known as **units** or **nodes**) in a neural network work together to learn from data and make predictions.

A neural network is made up of layers of interconnected neurons. Each neuron in one layer is connected to neurons in the next layer, creating a flow of information from input to output.

Simple Analogy:

Imagine you're trying to teach a robot to recognize objects. You show it pictures of cats and dogs, and each picture has a label ("cat" or "dog"). The robot looks at each picture and tries to find patterns that distinguish cats from dogs. Each layer of the neural network helps the robot learn increasingly complex patterns, from simple features like edges to more complex ones like ears and tails.

The process of training a neural network involves adjusting the connections (also known as **weights**) between the neurons so that the network gets better at making predictions.

Building Blocks of Neural Networks

At the core of every neural network are **neurons** (also called **nodes**). These neurons are the building blocks that process information, and they are organized into

layers. Let's take a closer look at the essential components of a neural network.

1. Neurons (Nodes):

Neurons are the fundamental units of a neural network. Each neuron receives one or more inputs, processes them, and then passes the result to the next layer.

- **Input**: Each neuron receives input, typically from previous neurons (or from the input layer in the case of the first layer).

- **Weights**: The input values are multiplied by **weights**, which determine the importance of each input.

- **Bias**: A bias term is added to the weighted sum of inputs, allowing the model to shift the activation function's output, providing flexibility.

- **Activation Function**: The output of the neuron is determined by applying an **activation function** to the weighted sum of inputs and bias. Common activation functions include **ReLU** (Rectified Linear Unit), **sigmoid**, and **tanh**.

2. Layers:

Neurons are organized into layers. These layers can be broadly categorized into three types:

- **Input Layer**: The first layer, which receives the input data (e.g., pixel values in an image).

- **Hidden Layers**: These layers are where the actual computation takes place. Each hidden layer applies the activation function to the weighted sum of inputs from the previous layer. A neural network can have one or more hidden layers.

- **Output Layer**: The final layer that provides the prediction (e.g., the class label for classification tasks).

3. Weights and Biases:

The connections between neurons are represented by **weights** that indicate how strongly one neuron influences another. The **bias** allows the model to adjust the output independently of the input, giving it more flexibility.

4. Training:

Training a neural network involves adjusting the weights and biases through a process called **backpropagation**. During backpropagation, the error (or difference between predicted and actual output) is propagated back through the network to adjust the weights, minimizing the error over time.

Types of Neural Networks

Neural networks come in many shapes and sizes, depending on the type of problem you are trying to solve. Below are some common types of neural networks:

1. Feedforward Neural Networks (FNN):

The simplest type of neural network, where information flows in one direction, from the input layer to the output layer, passing through hidden layers. There is no feedback loop, and data flows only forward through the network.

- **Use Case**: Basic classification problems like digit recognition, where the goal is to predict a class label from input data.

2. Convolutional Neural Networks (CNN):

Convolutional neural networks are specialized for processing grid-like data, such as images. They use **convolutional layers** that apply filters to the input data to detect local patterns like edges, textures, and shapes. CNNs are highly effective in image recognition tasks.

- **Use Case**: Image classification, object detection, and face recognition.

3. Recurrent Neural Networks (RNN):

Recurrent neural networks are designed for sequential data, where the output of one step is fed back into the model for the next step. This allows RNNs to capture temporal dependencies and patterns in time-series data or sequences, making them ideal for tasks involving sequential input.

- **Use Case**: Speech recognition, language translation, and time-series forecasting.

4. Generative Adversarial Networks (GANs):

GANs consist of two neural networks: a **generator** and a **discriminator**. The generator creates fake data, and the discriminator attempts to distinguish between real and fake data. The two networks are trained together in a game-theoretic setup, where the generator gets better at producing realistic data, and the discriminator gets better at detecting fake data.

- **Use Case**: Image generation, video synthesis, and data augmentation.

Real-World Examples of Neural Networks

Neural networks have been successfully applied to a variety of real-world problems, especially those involving large and complex datasets. Let's explore a few key examples.

1. Image Recognition (Self-Driving Cars):

Self-driving cars rely on neural networks to interpret images from cameras and make decisions. CNNs, in particular, are used to identify pedestrians, traffic signs, road lanes, and other objects on the road.

- **How It Works**: A CNN processes the raw image data, extracting features like edges, textures, and shapes. As the data moves through the layers, the model learns to recognize complex objects like cars, pedestrians, and stop signs.

The network then makes predictions, such as whether to stop at a red light or yield to pedestrians.

2. Voice Assistants (Speech-to-Text):

Voice assistants like **Siri, Alexa**, and **Google Assistant** use RNNs and other neural networks to process and convert spoken language into text.

- **How It Works**: When you speak into a voice assistant, the model processes the sound wave (converted into spectrograms or MFCC features), which is then passed through an RNN or a CNN. The model learns to map the audio to the corresponding text, enabling the assistant to understand commands and queries.

Hands-On Project: Building a Feedforward Neural Network to Classify Handwritten Digits (MNIST)

Now that we've covered the theory, let's dive into a hands-on project to build a simple **feedforward neural network** (FNN) for digit classification using the famous **MNIST dataset**. This dataset consists of

70,000 images of handwritten digits (0-9), each 28x28 pixels in size.

Step 1: Set Up the Environment

First, we need to install the necessary libraries. For this project, we'll use **TensorFlow** (which includes **Keras** for high-level API support) to build and train the model.

bash

```
pip install tensorflow
```

Step 2: Load the MNIST Dataset

TensorFlow provides an easy-to-use method to load the MNIST dataset.

python

```
import tensorflow as tf
from tensorflow.keras.datasets import mnist

# Load MNIST dataset
(X_train, y_train), (X_test, y_test) = mnist.load_data()
```

```python
# Normalize the data to values between 0 and 1

X_train, X_test = X_train / 255.0, X_test / 255.0


# Reshape the images to 1D arrays (28x28 to 784)

X_train = X_train.reshape(-1, 28 * 28)

X_test = X_test.reshape(-1, 28 * 28)
```

Step 3: Build the Neural Network Model

We'll create a basic feedforward neural network with one hidden layer.

python

```python
from tensorflow.keras.models import Sequential

from tensorflow.keras.layers import Dense


# Build the neural network model

model = Sequential([
```

```
Dense(128, activation='relu', input_shape=(784,)),  # Input
layer + hidden layer with 128 neurons

Dense(10, activation='softmax')  # Output layer with 10
neurons (one for each digit)

])
```

```
# Compile the model
model.compile(optimizer='adam',
loss='sparse_categorical_crossentropy', metrics=['accuracy'])
```

Step 4: Train the Model

Next, we'll train the model using the training data. We'll train for 5 epochs, which is typically sufficient to get a good result on MNIST.

python

```
# Train the model
model.fit(X_train, y_train, epochs=5)
```

Step 5: Evaluate the Model

After training, we'll evaluate the model on the test data to see how well it performs.

python

```python
# Evaluate the model on test data
test_loss, test_acc = model.evaluate(X_test, y_test)
print(f'Test accuracy: {test_acc}')
```

Step 6: Make Predictions

Finally, we can use the trained model to make predictions on new data.

python

```python
# Predict on test data
predictions = model.predict(X_test)

# Show the first predicted class
print(f'Predicted label for the first image: {predictions[0].argmax()}')
```

Conclusion

In this chapter, we've explored the fascinating world of **neural networks** and **deep learning**. From understanding the basic components of neural networks—such as neurons, layers, and activation functions—to learning about different types of neural networks like **feedforward**, **convolutional**, and **recurrent** networks, we've built a solid foundation in this powerful machine learning technique.

We also explored real-world applications, such as **image recognition** in self-driving cars and **speech-to-text** in voice assistants, to see how neural networks are being used to solve complex problems. Finally, we completed a hands-on project building a **feedforward neural network** to classify handwritten digits from the MNIST dataset, giving you a practical understanding of how to build and train neural networks.

Neural networks are the backbone of deep learning, and this chapter has equipped you with the knowledge to explore them further. With frameworks like **TensorFlow** and **PyTorch**, you now have the tools to experiment with more advanced architectures and apply deep learning to solve a wide range of real-world problems. The journey into deep learning is just beginning, and you're well on your way to mastering this exciting and transformative field.

Chapter 10: Practical Deep Learning Projects

Introduction

Deep learning has proven to be a powerful tool for solving complex problems across various domains, especially in fields such as computer vision, natural language processing (NLP), and time-series analysis. As deep learning models grow in complexity and size, they offer remarkable capabilities—from recognizing objects in images to predicting stock prices. However, while the potential is vast, the computational and data requirements for training deep learning models from scratch can be daunting.

That's where **transfer learning** and **fine-tuning** come in. These techniques allow you to leverage the power of pre-trained models, saving both time and computational resources while still achieving high accuracy on specific tasks. In this chapter, we will explore the practical application of deep learning techniques in **image recognition**, **text analysis**, and **time-series forecasting**. We'll take a hands-on approach by using pre-trained models and applying them to custom datasets.

By the end of this chapter, you will have a clear understanding of how to apply deep learning to real-world problems using frameworks like **TensorFlow** and **PyTorch**, without needing a massive dataset or computational resources to train a model from scratch.

Convolutional Neural Networks (CNNs) for Image Tasks

One of the most significant breakthroughs in deep learning is **Convolutional Neural Networks (CNNs)**, which have transformed the field of image recognition. CNNs excel at identifying spatial hierarchies in images—starting with simple patterns like edges and textures in the first layers, and building up to more complex patterns (such as faces or objects) in deeper layers. They are the workhorse behind technologies like facial recognition, object detection, and image classification.

How CNNs Work:

CNNs are composed of several different types of layers:

1. **Convolutional Layers**: These layers use **filters** (also known as **kernels**) to scan over the input image. The filter slides over the image, performing a **convolution** operation, which helps detect specific patterns, such as edges, textures, or more complex features.

2. **Activation Layers (ReLU)**: After each convolution, an activation function like **ReLU** (Rectified Linear Unit) is applied to introduce non-linearity to the model, helping it learn more complex patterns.

3. **Pooling Layers**: Pooling layers (such as **max pooling**) downsample the image, reducing its size while preserving important information. This step helps reduce computational cost and overfitting.

4. **Fully Connected Layers**: Towards the end of the CNN, fully connected layers (or dense layers) help the network make final predictions based on the learned features.

Why CNNs are Great for Images:

CNNs are particularly well-suited for image tasks because they take advantage of **spatial locality**. In images, pixels that are close together are often related to each other (e.g., neighboring pixels might form part of an object or edge). CNNs capture these local relationships through their convolutions, making them highly efficient for image recognition.

Real-World Example:

CNNs power many real-world applications, such as:

- **Self-driving cars**: Recognizing pedestrians, traffic signs, and other vehicles.

- **Medical imaging**: Detecting tumors in X-rays, MRIs, or CT scans.

- **Face recognition**: Identifying individuals in photos or video.

Transfer Learning: Using Pre-Trained Models to Save Time and Data

One of the biggest challenges in deep learning is the need for large amounts of data and significant computational resources to train models from scratch. **Transfer learning** is a technique that helps mitigate this by leveraging pre-trained models that have already been trained on large datasets (such as ImageNet, which contains millions of images across thousands of categories).

How Transfer Learning Works:

1. **Pre-trained models**: Transfer learning starts with a model that has been trained on a large, general dataset. The pre-trained model has already learned a variety of features that are useful for many tasks.

2. **Fine-tuning**: You take the pre-trained model and adapt it to your specific problem (e.g., classifying dog breeds). Fine-tuning involves re-training the model on your dataset, but instead of starting from scratch, you adjust the weights of the model based on the new data. You may also freeze some layers (usually the earlier

layers) that have learned useful general features, and only update the deeper layers.

3. **Feature extraction**: You can also use the pre-trained model as a feature extractor. This means you take the output from the layers before the final classification layer and use it as input to a simpler model, such as a linear classifier.

Why Transfer Learning Works:

Transfer learning is effective because it capitalizes on the idea that many low-level features learned from a large dataset (e.g., edges, textures) are transferable to other tasks. By leveraging the knowledge learned from large-scale datasets, transfer learning reduces the need for massive amounts of data and computational power.

Popular Pre-Trained Models:

Some widely used pre-trained models include:

- **VGG16**: A deep CNN model with 16 layers that is highly popular for image classification.

- **ResNet**: A model with **residual connections**, allowing for very deep architectures and better gradient flow, often used for complex image tasks.

- **MobileNet**: A lightweight model designed for mobile devices, offering a trade-off between accuracy and computational efficiency.

Recurrent Neural Networks (RNNs): A Brief Introduction for Text and Time-Series Data

While CNNs are fantastic for image-related tasks, there's a whole different class of neural networks designed for sequential data—**Recurrent Neural Networks (RNNs)**. These networks are built to handle data where the current input depends on previous inputs, making them well-suited for tasks such as text analysis, time-series forecasting, and speech recognition.

How RNNs Work:

RNNs introduce **feedback loops** into the network, where the output of a neuron is fed back into the input of the same neuron in the next time step. This allows

RNNs to **remember** information from previous steps in a sequence.

- **Hidden States**: RNNs maintain a hidden state, which carries information from previous time steps and affects the network's decision in the current step.

- **Vanishing Gradient Problem**: One challenge with traditional RNNs is the **vanishing gradient problem**, where the influence of earlier inputs becomes diminished as the sequence grows longer. To address this, advanced RNN architectures like **Long Short-Term Memory (LSTM)** and **Gated Recurrent Units (GRU)** were developed, which can capture long-term dependencies in sequences more effectively.

Real-World Applications of RNNs:

- **Text generation**: Models like GPT-3 and OpenAI's Transformer-based models use RNNs or similar architectures to generate human-like text.

- **Speech-to-text**: Converting spoken language into written text using sequential input from audio features.

- **Time-series forecasting**: Predicting stock prices, weather patterns, or sales trends based on historical data.

Hands-On Project: Fine-Tuning a Pre-Trained Image Classifier (MobileNet or ResNet)

In this project, we will take a **pre-trained image classifier** and fine-tune it for a custom task. Specifically, we'll classify **dog breeds** using a smaller dataset, leveraging the power of **transfer learning**.

Step 1: Set Up the Environment

First, install the necessary packages and frameworks. We'll use **TensorFlow** for this task, as it provides simple access to pre-trained models.

bash

pip install tensorflow

Step 2: Load and Preprocess the Dataset

For this project, we'll use a small dataset of images of different dog breeds. If you don't have a dataset of dog images, you can easily download one or use a sample dataset available in TensorFlow.

python

```
import tensorflow as tf

from tensorflow.keras.preprocessing.image import
ImageDataGenerator


# Define paths to the training and validation datasets

train_dir = "path_to_train_data"

valid_dir = "path_to_valid_data"


# Preprocess images with the ImageDataGenerator

train_datagen = ImageDataGenerator(rescale=1./255,
horizontal_flip=True)

valid_datagen = ImageDataGenerator(rescale=1./255)
```

train_generator = train_datagen.flow_from_directory(train_dir,

target_size=(224, 224), batch_size=32,

class_mode='categorical')

valid_generator = valid_datagen.flow_from_directory(valid_dir,

target_size=(224, 224), batch_size=32,

class_mode='categorical')

Step 3: Load a Pre-Trained Model (MobileNet or ResNet)

We'll use **MobileNet**, a lightweight CNN that's ideal for mobile applications but still powerful for image classification.

python

 # Load the pre-trained MobileNet model, excluding the final classification layer

base_model = tf.keras.applications.MobileNetV2(input_shape=(224, 224, 3), include_top=False, weights='imagenet')

 # Freeze the layers of the base model

```
base_model.trainable = False


# Add custom layers on top of MobileNet

model = tf.keras.Sequential([

    base_model,

    tf.keras.layers.GlobalAveragePooling2D(),

    tf.keras.layers.Dense(1024, activation='relu'),

    tf.keras.layers.Dense(10, activation='softmax')  # Assuming
10 dog breeds

])


# Compile the model

model.compile(optimizer='adam',
loss='categorical_crossentropy', metrics=['accuracy'])
```

Step 4: Train the Model

Now, we'll train the model using our custom dog breed dataset. Since we're fine-tuning a pre-trained model, we don't need a massive dataset to achieve good performance.

python

```
history = model.fit(
    train_generator,
    steps_per_epoch=train_generator.samples // 32,
    epochs=5,
    validation_data=valid_generator,
    validation_steps=valid_generator.samples // 32
)
```

Step 5: Evaluate and Fine-Tune

After training for a few epochs, we can evaluate the model's performance on the validation data. If necessary, we can unfreeze some of the layers in the base model and continue training to fine-tune the model further.

python

```
# Evaluate the model on the validation data
loss, accuracy = model.evaluate(valid_generator)
```

print(f"Validation Accuracy: {accuracy}")

 # Optionally, unfreeze some layers for further fine-tuning

base_model.trainable = True

for layer in base_model.layers[:-10]: # Freeze all but the last 10 layers

   layer.trainable = False

 # Re-compile and retrain the model

model.compile(optimizer=tf.keras.optimizers.Adam(learning_rate=1e-5), loss='categorical_crossentropy', metrics=['accuracy'])

model.fit(train_generator, epochs=5, validation_data=valid_generator)

Conclusion

In this chapter, we delved into the practical aspects of deep learning, focusing on how to leverage **pre-trained models** to solve real-world problems effectively, even with limited data. By using **transfer learning**, we were able to apply powerful neural networks like **MobileNet** to custom image classification tasks without requiring a massive dataset or extensive computational resources.

We also explored the world of **Convolutional Neural Networks (CNNs)**, which are at the heart of image recognition tasks, and **Recurrent Neural Networks (RNNs)**, which excel at sequential data like text and time-series. Through this hands-on project, you learned how to fine-tune a pre-trained model for a new task, allowing you to build a dog breed classifier with minimal effort.

This chapter has equipped you with the knowledge and practical experience to tackle deep learning problems across a range of domains, from image recognition to time-series forecasting. As you move forward, you can apply these concepts and techniques to your own projects, taking advantage of transfer learning to achieve impressive results without the need for vast amounts of data or computational power.

Chapter 11: Natural Language Processing (NLP) Made Accessible

Introduction

Natural Language Processing (NLP) is one of the most exciting areas of artificial intelligence (AI). It involves the interaction between computers and human language, allowing machines to understand, interpret, and generate text in a way that feels natural. With applications ranging from **chatbots** to **social media sentiment analysis**, NLP has the power to transform industries, enhance user experiences, and automate many tasks that once required human intelligence.

While NLP can appear complex due to the vast number of techniques and algorithms involved, the core concepts can be broken down and applied in practical ways. This chapter will demystify NLP by explaining the essential concepts, including **tokenization, word embeddings** (like Word2Vec, GloVe, and BERT), and simple text classification tasks such as **sentiment analysis**. We will also explore real-world applications like **chatbots, email tagging**, and **social media sentiment analysis**, helping you understand how NLP is changing the way we interact with machines.

By the end of this chapter, you'll be equipped to build your own NLP applications, using well-known libraries and pre-trained models. We will also go through a hands-on project, where you'll build a **sentiment analysis** model that can classify movie reviews or tweets as positive or negative.

What is Natural Language Processing?

NLP is a subfield of AI and linguistics that focuses on enabling machines to process and understand human language in a meaningful way. Human language is incredibly rich, complex, and often ambiguous, which makes it difficult for machines to comprehend without specialized techniques. NLP bridges this gap by teaching computers how to process text in ways that are useful for various applications.

NLP has many subfields, but some of the most common tasks include:

- **Tokenization**: Breaking text into individual words or subwords.

- **Text classification**: Assigning categories or labels to text, such as sentiment analysis or topic categorization.

- **Named Entity Recognition (NER)**: Identifying specific entities like names, dates, or locations in text.

- **Part-of-speech tagging**: Assigning grammatical categories (like nouns, verbs, and adjectives) to each word in a sentence.

- **Machine translation**: Automatically translating text from one language to another.

- **Text generation**: Generating new text that resembles a given input text.

In this chapter, we'll focus on two core components of NLP that are foundational to many NLP applications: **tokenization** and **word embeddings**. We'll also dive into a simple NLP task: **text classification**, which can be used to classify the sentiment of text (e.g., positive or negative).

Tokenization: The First Step in Text Processing

Tokenization is one of the most fundamental steps in NLP. It involves breaking down text into smaller, meaningful units called **tokens**. These tokens are often words, but they can also be subwords, sentences, or characters, depending on the level of tokenization.

Why Tokenization Is Important:

Text in its raw form, such as a string of characters, doesn't provide much value to a machine learning model. Tokenizing text helps convert it into discrete units that the model can process. For example:

- "I love this movie!" becomes the tokens: ["I", "love", "this", "movie", "!"]

- Tokenization allows the model to understand individual words and how they relate to one another, enabling the model to extract meaning.

Types of Tokenization:

1. **Word-level tokenization**: This approach splits text into individual words. For example, the sentence "I love NLP" would be tokenized as ["I", "love", "NLP"].

2. **Subword-level tokenization**: Some NLP tasks benefit from breaking words into smaller units, especially in languages with complex morphology or when handling unknown words. For example, "unhappiness" might be tokenized as ["un", "happiness"].

3. **Sentence-level tokenization**: This involves breaking text into sentences rather than individual words. This can be useful for tasks that need to understand sentence structure.

Common Tokenization Tools:

- **NLTK** (Natural Language Toolkit) and **spaCy** are two popular libraries for tokenization in Python.

- **Hugging Face Transformers** provides powerful tokenizers for modern language models like BERT.

Word Embeddings: Capturing the Meaning of Words

Once the text is tokenized, the next step is to convert these tokens into a format that can be understood by machine learning models. One of the most effective ways to represent words in a numerical format is through **word embeddings**. Word embeddings are vector representations of words that capture their meanings based on context.

Why Word Embeddings Matter:

Traditional methods of representing text, such as using **one-hot encoding**, create sparse and high-dimensional vectors that don't capture any semantic relationships between words. Word embeddings, on the other hand, are dense and low-dimensional, and more importantly, they capture the **semantic relationships** between words. For example, word embeddings for "king" and "queen" will be close in vector space because they share similar meanings.

Popular Word Embeddings:

1. **Word2Vec:** Word2Vec, developed by **Google**, is one of the most widely used techniques for creating word embeddings. It uses a shallow neural network to learn vector representations of words by predicting the context in which a word appears.

   - **Skip-gram model:** The model learns to predict surrounding words based on the given word.

   - **Continuous Bag of Words (CBOW):** The model learns to predict a word based on its surrounding context.

2. **GloVe (Global Vectors for Word Representation):** GloVe, developed by **Stanford**, is another popular word embedding technique. Unlike Word2Vec, which uses local context to learn word representations, GloVe constructs word vectors by aggregating global word-word co-occurrence statistics from a corpus.

3. **BERT (Bidirectional Encoder Representations from Transformers):** BERT is a more recent and

advanced model that uses a transformer architecture to learn contextual word representations. Unlike Word2Vec and GloVe, which generate static embeddings, BERT generates **contextual embeddings**—meaning the embedding for a word changes depending on its surrounding context. BERT has become one of the most powerful models for many NLP tasks, including text classification, sentiment analysis, and question answering.

Simple Text Classification: Sentiment Analysis

One of the most common tasks in NLP is **text classification**, where the goal is to categorize text into predefined classes. A popular example of text classification is **sentiment analysis**, where the model predicts whether a piece of text expresses a positive, negative, or neutral sentiment.

How Sentiment Analysis Works:

1. **Data Preprocessing**: The first step in sentiment analysis is to preprocess the text data, which typically involves cleaning the text, tokenizing it,

and converting it into numerical representations (such as word embeddings).

2. **Feature Extraction**: This step involves extracting meaningful features from the text. This could involve using techniques like **TF-IDF** (Term Frequency-Inverse Document Frequency) or applying word embeddings like Word2Vec or GloVe.

3. **Model Training**: Once the features are extracted, a machine learning model (such as a **logistic regression, SVM,** or **neural network**) is trained on labeled data to classify the sentiment.

4. **Prediction**: After training, the model can predict the sentiment of new, unseen text.

Real-World Example:

Sentiment analysis is widely used to analyze customer feedback, social media posts, product reviews, and more. It can help businesses understand how their customers feel about their products or services and make data-driven decisions.

Real-World Use Cases for NLP

NLP is used in a wide range of real-world applications that impact everyday life. Let's look at some prominent examples:

1. Chatbots:

Chatbots use NLP to simulate conversation with human users. They process user inputs, understand the intent behind the message, and generate an appropriate response. Popular examples include customer service bots on websites or virtual assistants like **Siri** and **Alexa**.

2. Social Media Sentiment Analysis:

NLP is frequently used to analyze sentiments expressed on social media platforms like Twitter, Facebook, or Instagram. Sentiment analysis helps brands understand public opinion, identify potential crises, and improve customer engagement.

- **Use Case**: A company might use sentiment analysis to monitor social media posts about its new product launch and gather real-time feedback.

3. Email Tagging:

NLP is often used for email classification tasks. For example, companies use NLP to categorize incoming emails into folders (e.g., "spam," "important," or "promotions") or to prioritize urgent messages.

Hands-On Project: Building a Sentiment Analyzer on Movie Reviews or Tweets

Now that we have a solid understanding of the core concepts in NLP, let's dive into a practical project. We will build a simple **sentiment analyzer** using preprocessed movie reviews or tweets and train a model to classify them as positive or negative.

Step 1: Set Up the Environment

We will use **TensorFlow** and **Keras** to build our model. You'll need to install the necessary libraries:

bash

pip install tensorflow

For this project, we'll use the **IMDb dataset** for movie reviews, but you can adapt the steps to work with tweets or any other textual data.

Step 2: Load and Preprocess the Dataset

We'll start by loading the **IMDb dataset**, which is already preprocessed for sentiment analysis. It contains 50,000 movie reviews labeled as positive or negative.

python

```
import tensorflow as tf

from tensorflow.keras.datasets import imdb

from tensorflow.keras.preprocessing.sequence import pad_sequences


# Load the IMDb dataset

(x_train, y_train), (x_test, y_test) = imdb.load_data(num_words=10000)


# Pad sequences to ensure equal length
```

x_train = pad_sequences(x_train, maxlen=500)

x_test = pad_sequences(x_test, maxlen=500)

Step 3: Build the Sentiment Analysis Model

We'll build a simple **feedforward neural network** to classify the reviews as positive or negative.

python

```
from tensorflow.keras.models import Sequential

from tensorflow.keras.layers import Dense, Embedding,
GlobalAveragePooling1D


# Build the model

model = Sequential([

    Embedding(input_dim=10000, output_dim=128,
input_length=500),

    GlobalAveragePooling1D(),

    Dense(16, activation='relu'),

    Dense(1, activation='sigmoid')  # Binary output: positive (1)
or negative (0)
```

])

 # Compile the model

model.compile(optimizer='adam', loss='binary_crossentropy', metrics=['accuracy'])

Step 4: Train the Model

We'll now train the model on the training data.

python

history = model.fit(x_train, y_train, epochs=5, batch_size=64, validation_data=(x_test, y_test))

Step 5: Evaluate and Interpret the Results

After training the model, we can evaluate its performance on the test data.

python

 # Evaluate the model on the test data

loss, accuracy = model.evaluate(x_test, y_test)

print(f"Test Accuracy: {accuracy}")

Step 6: Make Predictions

Finally, we'll use the trained model to make predictions on new, unseen data.

python

```
# Predict sentiment for the first review in the test set

prediction = model.predict(x_test[0:1])

print(f"Predicted sentiment: {'Positive' if prediction > 0.5 else 'Negative'}")
```

Conclusion

In this chapter, we've broken down the complexities of **Natural Language Processing (NLP)** into digestible concepts. We explored the essentials of **tokenization**, **word embeddings** (like Word2Vec, GloVe, and BERT), and **simple text classification** (such as sentiment analysis). These techniques are foundational for many NLP tasks, including **chatbots, social media sentiment analysis**, and **email tagging**.

Through a hands-on project, we demonstrated how to build a simple **sentiment analyzer** using preprocessed movie reviews from the IMDb dataset. We walked through each training step, from preprocessing and tokenizing the text to training and evaluating the model.

With this knowledge, you now have the tools to apply NLP techniques to a wide range of text-based tasks. Whether you're analyzing customer feedback, building a chatbot, or monitoring social media trends, NLP provides powerful capabilities for understanding and interacting with human language.

Chapter 12: Human-Robot Interaction (HRI) and Machine Learning

Introduction

In recent years, robots have evolved from machines confined to factory floors into highly interactive entities that can collaborate with humans in a variety of settings. From **healthcare** to **hospitality**, robots are now designed to not only carry out tasks but also engage with people in a meaningful way. This progress is largely due to advances in **machine learning (ML)**, which allows robots to perceive the world around them, understand human intentions, and respond in an intelligent, adaptive manner.

Human-Robot Interaction (HRI) is a field of study that focuses on the interaction between humans and robots. As robots become more intelligent and capable of perceiving and interacting with humans, HRI has become essential to designing robots that can collaborate effectively, enhancing their usefulness in industries such as healthcare, manufacturing, and home assistance.

This chapter will delve into how **machine learning** powers HRI systems, particularly in areas like **vision**, **speech recognition**, **gesture recognition**, and **reinforcement learning** for robotic control. We will explore real-world examples of robots in action, from **collaborative robots (cobots)** in manufacturing to **service robots** in hotels. Finally, you'll get hands-on experience by training a virtual robot in a simple reinforcement learning environment to navigate a maze or balance a cart-pole.

By the end of this chapter, you will have a deep understanding of the principles of HRI and how machine learning is used to make robots smarter, more autonomous, and capable of collaborating with humans in real-world settings.

How ML Powers Robots to Perceive and Interact with Humans

One of the defining features of intelligent robots is their ability to perceive their environment and understand human behavior. **Machine learning** enables robots to interpret visual, auditory, and motion data to respond in an appropriate manner. These capabilities are essential for robots that are meant to collaborate or interact with humans, whether it's through **voice commands**, **gesture recognition**, or **facial expressions**.

1. Vision: Enabling Robots to See and Understand the World

Robots with **computer vision** capabilities can interpret visual data from cameras and other sensors to understand the environment. Machine learning algorithms, especially **deep learning** models like **Convolutional Neural Networks (CNNs)**, have revolutionized computer vision by allowing robots to recognize objects, people, and spatial relationships.

- **Object Recognition**: Robots can use ML algorithms to identify objects in their environment. For example, in a healthcare setting, a robot could be trained to recognize medical instruments, patient files, and even people's faces.

- **Depth Perception**: With stereo cameras or depth sensors like **LiDAR**, robots can perceive distances between objects and themselves, allowing for navigation and interaction with humans in a dynamic environment.

- **Facial Recognition**: Machine learning allows robots to recognize and remember human faces, enabling them to greet people, understand their emotions, or identify patients in healthcare settings.

2. Speech: Understanding and Responding to Human Language

Speech recognition is another area where ML is making a significant impact. Using **natural language processing (NLP)** and **deep learning models** like **transformers** (e.g., BERT, GPT), robots can understand spoken language and generate appropriate responses.

- **Voice Commands**: Robots in **home automation** or **hospitality** can respond to voice commands, such as turning on lights, setting an alarm, or offering assistance with tasks.

- **Speech-to-Text and Text-to-Speech**: These systems allow robots to process spoken language, convert it into text, and then respond verbally, creating a more interactive experience. Voice assistants like **Alexa** and **Siri** are popular examples of this technology.

- **Emotion Detection**: Through analyzing the tone and cadence of speech, robots can detect emotions and respond accordingly. For example, a robot in a healthcare setting might recognize a patient's distress through the tone of their voice and offer comforting words.

3. Gesture Recognition: Enabling Non-Verbal Interaction

Gestures are a fundamental part of human communication, and robots are increasingly being designed to recognize and respond to these gestures. **Machine learning models** are trained to identify specific motions and interpret their meanings, allowing robots to engage in a more natural, human-like manner.

- **Hand Gestures**: Using cameras or motion sensors, robots can recognize hand gestures such as pointing or waving. For example, a robot might interpret a raised hand as a request for attention or assistance.

- **Body Language**: More advanced robots can recognize entire body movements, including posture and walking patterns, to understand a person's intent. For instance, in a **healthcare setting**, a robot could track a patient's gait and detect signs of discomfort or imbalance.

Designing Robots That Collaborate Effectively with People

The ultimate goal of HRI is to design robots that can effectively collaborate with humans in diverse environments. For robots to work alongside people, they must understand human intentions, predict human actions, and adjust their behavior accordingly. Machine learning is central to this process, enabling robots to adapt to the unpredictable nature of human behavior.

1. Social Robots in Healthcare

Social robots are robots designed to interact with people in a friendly and supportive way, often used in contexts like **elderly care**, **therapy**, or **mental health support**. These robots must not only perform physical tasks but also communicate effectively with patients, showing empathy and understanding.

- **Example**: Robots like **Pepper** and **Mabu** are designed to interact with patients in hospitals, providing reminders for medication, engaging in conversation, and even recognizing emotional states to offer comfort.

2. Robots in Hospitality and Customer Service

Robots are also being used in **customer service** settings such as hotels, airports, and restaurants. These robots need to be able to understand customer queries, provide assistance, and work alongside human staff members to create a seamless experience.

- **Example**: Robots like **Relay** (used in hotels) deliver items to guests while navigating through hallways, avoiding obstacles, and interacting with customers using voice and touch interfaces. These robots leverage machine learning for navigation, speech recognition, and task management.

3. Collaborative Robots (Cobots) in Manufacturing

Collaborative robots (cobots) are designed to work side by side with human workers in manufacturing environments. Unlike traditional industrial robots, which are isolated from human workers for safety, cobots are designed to collaborate and assist with tasks like assembly, quality control, and packaging.

- **Example:** In a **manufacturing facility**, a robot might help a worker by holding a part in place while the worker fastens it. The robot uses machine learning for real-time decision-making, adjusting its actions based on the worker's movements.

Basics of Reinforcement Learning for Robotic Control

While **supervised learning** and **unsupervised learning** are commonly used for tasks like object recognition and speech processing, **reinforcement learning (RL)** is particularly useful for teaching robots how to perform tasks that require **decision-making** in dynamic, uncertain environments.

What is Reinforcement Learning?

Reinforcement learning is an area of machine learning where an agent (the robot) learns to make decisions by interacting with its environment. The agent takes actions and receives feedback from the environment in the form of rewards or penalties. Over time, the agent learns to maximize cumulative rewards, improving its performance in the task at hand.

- **Example**: A robot learning to navigate a maze or balance on a pole is using reinforcement learning. The robot gets a positive reward for moving in the right direction and a penalty for making incorrect moves.

How It Works:

1. **Agent**: The robot, which learns by interacting with its environment.

2. **Environment**: The surroundings or scenario in which the robot operates (e.g., a maze, a cart-pole).

3. **Actions**: The possible decisions or movements the robot can make.

4. **Rewards**: Feedback that the robot receives after taking an action. A positive reward encourages the robot to repeat the action, while a penalty discourages it.

Reinforcement Learning Algorithms:

- **Q-Learning**: A model-free RL algorithm where the agent learns an action-value function to estimate the reward for each action taken in a particular state.

- **Deep Q-Networks (DQN)**: Combines Q-learning with deep learning to handle large state spaces by using a deep neural network to approximate the Q-values.

Real-World Examples of Reinforcement Learning in Robotics

Reinforcement learning has been successfully applied in various real-world robotic systems, enabling robots to learn complex behaviors autonomously.

- **Autonomous Vehicles**: Self-driving cars use RL to learn how to navigate through traffic, make decisions at intersections, and avoid obstacles.

- **Warehouse Robots**: Robots in warehouses use RL to optimize tasks like picking and placing items, adjusting their movements based on real-time data from the environment.

- **Humanoid Robots**: Advanced robots like **Boston Dynamics' Atlas** use RL for learning complex movements such as walking, running, and balancing.

Hands-On Project: Reinforcement Learning with OpenAI Gym

Now that we've explored the basics of reinforcement learning, let's put this knowledge into practice by training a virtual robot to complete a task using the **OpenAI Gym** environment. OpenAI Gym provides a collection of environments where you can test and train reinforcement learning algorithms.

Step 1: Set Up the Environment

First, we need to install **OpenAI Gym** and **TensorFlow**.

bash

pip install gym

pip install tensorflow

Step 2: Set Up the CartPole Environment

The **CartPole** environment in OpenAI Gym is a classic reinforcement learning task where the goal is to balance a pole on top of a cart. The cart can move left or right, and the agent (the robot) needs to learn how to keep the pole balanced.

python

import gym

 # Create the CartPole environment

env = gym.make('CartPole-v1')

Reset the environment to start a new episode

state = env.reset()

Step 3: Define the Agent and Reward System

For this basic example, we'll use a simple RL agent that learns by trial and error. The agent will take actions (move left or right) and receive rewards based on its ability to keep the pole balanced.

python

```python
import numpy as np


# Simple Q-learning parameters
alpha = 0.1  # learning rate
gamma = 0.99  # discount factor
epsilon = 0.1  # exploration rate


# Q-table initialization
Q = np.zeros([env.observation_space.shape[0],
env.action_space.n])
```

```python
# Define the agent's action choice

def choose_action(state):

    if np.random.rand() < epsilon:

        return env.action_space.sample()  # Exploration

    else:

        return np.argmax(Q[state])  # Exploitation
```

Step 4: Train the Agent

Now, we'll train the agent over multiple episodes, updating the Q-table with each step.

python

```python
for episode in range(1000):  # number of episodes

    state = env.reset()

    done = False

    total_reward = 0


    while not done:
```

```
action = choose_action(state)

next_state, reward, done, _ = env.step(action)


# Q-learning update rule

Q[state, action] = Q[state, action] + alpha * (reward +
gamma * np.max(Q[next_state]) - Q[state, action])


state = next_state

total_reward += reward


if episode % 100 == 0:

print(f"Episode {episode}, Total Reward: {total_reward}")
```

Step 5: Evaluate the Agent's Performance

After training, we can evaluate how well the agent learned to balance the pole.

python

```
state = env.reset()
```

```
done = False

total_reward = 0


while not done:

    action = np.argmax(Q[state])

    state, reward, done, _ = env.step(action)

    total_reward += reward


print(f"Total Reward after training: {total_reward}")
```

Conclusion

In this chapter, we explored how **machine learning** and **reinforcement learning** are used to create intelligent robots capable of interacting with humans in meaningful ways. We learned how robots can perceive their environment using **vision**, **speech recognition**, and **gesture recognition**, and how they can respond to human behavior in a collaborative setting. By leveraging **machine learning**, robots can continuously improve their interactions with humans in dynamic environments.

We also introduced **reinforcement learning** as a method for training robots to make decisions based on feedback from their environment. Through the hands-on project, you gained practical experience with a reinforcement learning environment using **OpenAI Gym** to train a virtual robot to balance a cart-pole.

The principles and techniques covered in this chapter form the foundation for designing robots that can work seamlessly with humans in a variety of domains, from **healthcare** to **manufacturing** and beyond. With machine learning, robots are becoming more adaptable, capable, and collaborative, opening up new possibilities for their application in everyday life.

Chapter 13: Real-World Case Studies in Key Industries

Introduction

Machine learning (ML) has found its way into nearly every industry, driving innovation, improving efficiency, and enabling businesses to leverage data in ways never imagined before. Whether it's detecting early signs of failure in manufacturing equipment, predicting patient risk in healthcare, or optimizing delivery routes in logistics, machine learning is transforming the way industries operate. In this chapter, we will dive into **real-world case studies** across three key industries: **Manufacturing**, **Healthcare**, and **Logistics**. We'll explore how ML is applied to solve industry-specific problems, discuss the challenges unique to each domain, and provide actionable insights on how to plan, execute, and deploy ML projects.

We'll also walk through a **hands-on project**, guiding you through a simplified case study that demonstrates how to structure an ML project from start to finish—using publicly available data to forecast demand for a small delivery service. By the end of this chapter, you will have a deep understanding of how ML can be applied in practice and the steps involved in driving real-world projects to success.

Manufacturing: Predictive Maintenance and Supply Chain Optimization

Manufacturing is an industry that has seen a significant transformation with the advent of machine learning. By utilizing predictive analytics, manufacturers can reduce downtime, improve efficiency, and enhance product quality. Here are two key areas where machine learning is making a major impact:

1. Predictive Maintenance (Early Fault Detection)

Predictive maintenance uses machine learning to predict when equipment will fail or require maintenance, allowing businesses to schedule repairs before costly breakdowns occur. This minimizes unplanned downtime and reduces maintenance costs.

How It Works:

Predictive maintenance relies on data from sensors embedded in machines to monitor their condition. These sensors collect data such as temperature, vibration, and pressure, which can indicate whether a machine is operating within normal parameters. Machine learning algorithms are trained on this data to predict potential failures based on patterns and trends.

- **Anomaly Detection**: Machine learning models, such as **Random Forests** or **Support Vector Machines**, can be used to detect outliers in the data, signaling potential issues.

- **Time Series Forecasting**: Models like **ARIMA** (AutoRegressive Integrated Moving Average) and **LSTM** (Long Short-Term Memory) networks can predict future performance and maintenance needs based on historical data.

Real-World Example:

In a **factory** that uses industrial machinery, sensors might track the temperature of a motor. A machine learning model could detect that the temperature is rising unusually high and predict an impending failure, prompting maintenance before the motor breaks down, preventing costly downtime.

2. Supply Chain Optimization

In **supply chain optimization**, machine learning helps companies manage inventory, demand forecasting, and distribution to improve efficiency and reduce costs.

How It Works:

- **Demand Forecasting**: Machine learning algorithms like **XGBoost, Gradient Boosting Machines**, and **ARIMA** are used to forecast product demand based on historical sales data, market trends, and other factors.

- **Inventory Optimization**: ML models can also predict the optimal amount of stock to maintain at various locations, ensuring a balance between supply and demand.

- **Route Optimization**: Machine learning is used to calculate the most efficient routes for distribution trucks, factoring in variables such as traffic, weather, and delivery time windows.

Real-World Example:

A global retail chain might use predictive models to forecast the demand for a particular product in various regions, ensuring they have enough inventory in each warehouse. Additionally, route optimization models can help delivery trucks take the fastest paths to avoid delays.

Healthcare: Disease Prediction and Patient Risk Scoring

In the **healthcare** industry, machine learning has the potential to dramatically improve patient outcomes, reduce costs, and increase operational efficiency. Two key applications of ML in healthcare include **disease prediction** and **patient risk scoring**.

1. Disease Prediction

Machine learning models can analyze medical data to predict the likelihood of disease in patients, allowing for earlier interventions and better preventative care.

How It Works:

ML models are trained on historical patient data, including **electronic health records (EHRs)**, medical imaging, lab results, and genetic information. By identifying patterns and correlations in this data, ML models can predict the onset of conditions such as diabetes, cancer, heart disease, and other chronic illnesses.

- **Supervised Learning**: Algorithms like **Logistic Regression, Decision Trees**, and **Random Forests** can be used to predict disease risk based on labeled datasets of patients with known outcomes.

- **Deep Learning**: For tasks like **medical image analysis**, deep learning models such as **CNNs (Convolutional Neural Networks)** are used to detect anomalies in images, like tumors or lesions in X-rays, CT scans, or MRIs.

Real-World Example:

A machine learning model could be trained on historical medical data to predict the likelihood of a patient developing type 2 diabetes. This could help healthcare providers target at-risk individuals with preventative treatments and lifestyle changes before the disease develops.

2. Patient Risk Scoring

Patient risk scoring is the practice of evaluating patients based on their risk for adverse health outcomes, such as hospital readmission or complications after surgery. Machine learning models can assist in scoring patients by analyzing various factors, including their medical history, demographics, and lifestyle choices.

How It Works:

ML models are trained on data about patients who have experienced specific outcomes, allowing the model to recognize patterns and make predictions. For instance, a model might predict the likelihood that a patient will be readmitted to the hospital after discharge based on factors like age, previous hospitalizations, and comorbidities.

- **Ensemble Methods**: Random Forests and Gradient Boosting Machines are commonly used for risk scoring, as they can handle the complex, multi-dimensional nature of healthcare data.

- **Survival Analysis**: Techniques like **Cox Proportional Hazards Models** or **Random Survival Forests** can be used for predicting the time to an event, such as a patient's likelihood of experiencing a health complication.

Real-World Example:

A healthcare provider might use a machine learning model to score the risk of patients being readmitted to the hospital within 30 days after discharge. High-risk patients could be flagged for additional care or follow-up visits to reduce readmissions and improve outcomes.

Logistics: Route Optimization and Demand Forecasting

The **logistics** industry is another key area where machine learning is making a significant impact. From optimizing delivery routes to forecasting demand, ML has the potential to streamline operations, reduce costs, and improve customer satisfaction.

1. Route Optimization

One of the biggest challenges in logistics is **optimizing routes** for delivery vehicles, especially when dealing with large fleets and complex delivery networks. Machine learning algorithms can help identify the fastest, most cost-efficient routes, taking into account factors like traffic, weather, delivery time windows, and fuel consumption.

How It Works:

- **Vehicle Routing Problems (VRP)**: ML models are often used to solve VRP, where the goal is to determine the best routes for multiple vehicles to deliver goods to a set of destinations.

- **Reinforcement Learning**: In real-time delivery systems, reinforcement learning (RL) can be used to continuously optimize routes as new information becomes available, such as real-time traffic conditions.

Real-World Example:

A delivery company might use machine learning models to optimize routes for delivery trucks in a city. By analyzing traffic patterns and adjusting delivery schedules in real time, the company can minimize delivery times and fuel costs.

2. Demand Forecasting

Accurate **demand forecasting** is crucial in logistics to ensure that the right products are available at the right time and place. ML models can predict the demand for products at different locations and times, helping companies maintain optimal inventory levels and reduce waste.

How It Works:

- **Time Series Analysis**: Time series models like **ARIMA** and **LSTM** networks can be used to predict future demand based on historical data.

- **Factor Models**: By incorporating external factors like weather, holidays, or economic indicators, machine learning models can enhance forecasting accuracy.

Real-World Example:

An online retailer might use demand forecasting models to predict which products will experience spikes in demand during peak seasons, ensuring they have enough stock in warehouses across the country without overstocking.

Actionable Insights: Handling Industry-Specific Challenges

While machine learning offers great potential, each industry presents unique challenges that must be considered when planning and deploying an ML project. Below are some key considerations for implementing ML in the **manufacturing**, **healthcare**, and **logistics** industries:

1. Privacy and Security in Healthcare

Healthcare data is highly sensitive, and it is subject to strict regulations such as the **Health Insurance Portability and Accountability Act (HIPAA)** in the U.S. When working with medical data, it is crucial to ensure that patient privacy is protected at all stages of the project, from data collection to model deployment. Anonymizing data, encrypting sensitive information, and ensuring compliance with legal standards are essential steps.

2. Handling Large-Scale Data in Logistics

Logistics companies often deal with large volumes of data from multiple sources, including **GPS devices**, **traffic sensors**, and **inventory management systems**. Efficiently managing, processing, and analyzing this data requires robust infrastructure, including cloud-based solutions, distributed computing, and scalable machine learning pipelines.

3. Model Interpretability in Healthcare

In healthcare, the stakes are high, and model interpretability is crucial. Physicians need to understand why a machine learning model is recommending a certain treatment or predicting a particular outcome. **Explainable AI (XAI)** techniques, such as **LIME** (Local Interpretable Model-Agnostic Explanations) and **SHAP** (SHapley Additive exPlanations), are essential for ensuring that healthcare professionals can trust and act on model predictions.

Hands-On Project: Forecasting Demand for a Small Delivery Service

In this project, we will work through a simplified case study using publicly available data. We'll forecast demand for a small delivery service, helping us understand the process of building a machine learning model, from problem definition to deployment.

Step 1: Define the Problem

The goal of this project is to predict the demand for deliveries based on historical data. The company wants to predict the number of deliveries required on any given day to optimize its fleet management.

Step 2: Collect and Preprocess Data

We'll use publicly available **sales** and **weather data** as input features. These factors affect delivery demand, with higher demand typically occurring during peak times or bad weather.

python

```
import pandas as pd
```

```
# Load dataset

df = pd.read_csv('delivery_data.csv')


# Preprocess the data: handle missing values, convert date
columns, etc.

df['date'] = pd.to_datetime(df['date'])

df = df.fillna(method='ffill')
```

Step 3: Feature Engineering

We'll extract relevant features from the data, such as **day of the week, temperature,** and **holiday status,** which influence demand.

python

```
# Feature engineering: extract day of the week and other
relevant features

df['day_of_week'] = df['date'].dt.dayofweek

df['is_holiday'] = df['date'].isin(holidays).astype(int)
```

Step 4: Build the Model

We'll use a simple **Linear Regression** model to predict demand, but more advanced models like **Random Forests** or **XGBoost** can also be used for higher accuracy.

python

```python
from sklearn.model_selection import train_test_split

from sklearn.linear_model import LinearRegression

from sklearn.metrics import mean_absolute_error


# Split the data into training and testing sets

X = df[['day_of_week', 'temperature', 'is_holiday']]

y = df['demand']

X_train, X_test, y_train, y_test = train_test_split(X, y, test_size=0.2, random_state=42)


# Train the model

model = LinearRegression()
```

```
model.fit(X_train, y_train)


# Evaluate the model

predictions = model.predict(X_test)

mae = mean_absolute_error(y_test, predictions)

print(f'Mean Absolute Error: {mae}')
```

Step 5: Deploy the Model

Once the model is trained and evaluated, the next step would be to deploy it in a production environment. This could involve integrating the model into the company's operations dashboard, where it can automatically generate daily demand forecasts.

Conclusion

In this chapter, we explored **real-world case studies** of machine learning applications in key industries like **manufacturing, healthcare**, and **logistics**. By focusing on **predictive maintenance, supply chain optimization, disease prediction**, and **patient risk scoring**, we demonstrated how machine learning is transforming business operations, improving efficiency, and enhancing decision-making processes across these industries.

We also provided actionable insights on the unique challenges that arise when working with **industry-specific data**, such as **privacy concerns** in healthcare and **large-scale data management** in logistics. Finally, through a hands-on project, we walked you through the process of building a **demand forecasting model** for a small delivery service, demonstrating how to structure a machine learning project from problem definition to deployment.

Machine learning has the power to revolutionize industries, and by applying the principles outlined in this chapter, you can start building impactful solutions that drive real-world success.

Chapter 14: Ethical Considerations, Bias, and Responsible AI

Introduction

As machine learning (ML) and artificial intelligence (AI) become more pervasive across industries, the importance of addressing **ethical considerations** has never been more crucial. The decisions that ML models make can have significant consequences on individuals and communities, impacting everything from hiring decisions to healthcare outcomes to credit scores. If not carefully managed, AI systems can unintentionally perpetuate or even exacerbate existing biases, leading to unfair or discriminatory outcomes. Moreover, the lack of transparency and interpretability in AI systems can erode trust and accountability, particularly when these systems make high-stakes decisions.

This chapter will explore the ethical considerations surrounding AI, including **bias** in datasets and models, **privacy concerns**, **data security**, and the importance of **responsible AI** practices. We'll also delve into **explainability and transparency** in machine learning, emphasizing how to ensure that AI models remain interpretable and accountable. Real-world examples will highlight the ethical challenges posed by AI, such as **biased facial recognition systems** and **credit scoring controversies**.

By the end of this chapter, you will not only understand the key ethical issues in AI but also be equipped with practical tools and checklists for **mitigating bias** and ensuring that your AI models are fair, transparent, and responsible. We'll also walk through a hands-on project to demonstrate how to check for bias in a classification dataset, measure disparities between different groups, and explore potential fixes.

Recognizing and Mitigating Bias in Datasets and Models

Bias in AI is not just a theoretical concern—it has real-world implications. **Bias** refers to the systematic error introduced by AI models that can lead to unfair or unequal outcomes for different individuals or groups. Machine learning models are only as good as the data they are trained on, and if that data is biased or unrepresentative, the model will learn and perpetuate these biases. Understanding and mitigating bias is key to developing ethical AI systems.

Types of Bias in AI:

1. **Data Bias**: Data bias occurs when the data used to train the model is unrepresentative of the real world. This can happen when the dataset over-represents certain groups or under-represents others, leading to biased predictions.

   o **Example**: If a facial recognition model is trained primarily on images of white individuals, it may perform poorly on individuals of other races, exhibiting racial bias.

2. **Sampling Bias**: Sampling bias happens when the data used for training is not randomly selected and does not accurately represent the entire population.

   ○ **Example**: If a healthcare model is trained on data from a specific geographic region or demographic group, it may not perform well for patients outside that region or group.

3. **Label Bias**: Label bias occurs when the labels assigned to data are influenced by human prejudices or societal stereotypes.

   ○ **Example**: In a criminal justice dataset, if judges or police officers label certain behaviors as more "criminal" based on stereotypes, the model will learn those biases and perpetuate them.

How to Mitigate Bias:

1. **Diverse and Representative Data**: Ensure that the dataset is representative of all demographic groups and reflects the diversity of the population. This can involve oversampling underrepresented groups or collecting more

data from areas or communities that are often excluded.

2. **Fairness Constraints**: Implement fairness constraints during model training to ensure that the model performs equally well for all groups. This can be done by applying **adversarial debiasing** techniques or using fairness metrics such as **demographic parity** or **equalized odds**.

3. **Bias Audits**: Regularly conduct **bias audits** on your models to check for disparities in performance between different demographic groups. These audits can help identify hidden biases and provide insights into how to adjust the model for fairness.

Privacy Concerns, Data Security, and Responsible AI Guidelines

As AI systems increasingly rely on personal data, ensuring that this data is handled responsibly is critical. Privacy concerns and data security are at the forefront of responsible AI development, especially when it comes to sensitive information like health records, financial data, and personal identifiers.

Privacy Concerns:

1. **Data Minimization**: Collect only the data that is necessary for the task at hand. Avoid collecting unnecessary personal information that could be used to identify individuals or violate their privacy.

2. **Anonymization**: Anonymize sensitive data wherever possible, ensuring that any personal identifiers are removed before using the data for training. **Differential privacy** is one method used to add noise to the data in a way that prevents the identification of individuals, while still allowing for meaningful analysis.

3. **Informed Consent**: Ensure that individuals whose data is being used for training AI models provide **informed consent**, meaning they understand how their data will be used, stored, and shared.

Data Security:

1. **Encryption**: Encrypt sensitive data both during transmission and at rest to ensure that it is protected from unauthorized access.

2. **Access Control**: Implement strict access controls to ensure that only authorized personnel can access sensitive data, reducing the risk of data breaches.

3. **Secure Machine Learning**: Secure machine learning practices, such as **secure multi-party computation (SMPC)** and **federated learning**, allow models to be trained on data without directly accessing the sensitive information, ensuring privacy.

Responsible AI Guidelines:

1. **Transparency**: Maintain transparency in how models are trained, what data is used, and how decisions are made. This helps build trust in AI systems and ensures accountability.

2. **Accountability**: Ensure that there is a clear line of accountability for the decisions made by AI systems. Organizations should be responsible for the outcomes of their models and should

have mechanisms in place to rectify mistakes or biases that emerge.

3. **Ethical Review**: Implement an **ethical review process** during the development of AI systems, where a diverse team of experts reviews the models for fairness, transparency, and ethical considerations.

Explainability and Transparency in Machine Learning

As AI models become more complex, particularly with the rise of deep learning and neural networks, ensuring that these models remain interpretable and transparent has become a key challenge. **Model explainability** is essential for gaining the trust of users and stakeholders, particularly when the models are making decisions that impact people's lives.

Why Explainability Matters:

- **Trust**: Users need to trust the decisions made by AI systems, especially when those decisions have significant impacts. For example, in healthcare, patients and doctors need to understand how an AI system arrived at a diagnosis or treatment recommendation.

- **Accountability**: In high-stakes applications like criminal justice or finance, it's important to understand why a model made a particular decision to ensure fairness and prevent discrimination.

- **Improvement**: Explainability allows data scientists to understand how a model works, identify weaknesses, and improve its performance.

Techniques for Explainable AI:

1. **LIME (Local Interpretable Model-Agnostic Explanations)**: LIME explains individual predictions by approximating the black-box model with an interpretable model on a locally defined dataset. This helps understand why a model made a particular prediction for a given instance.

2. **SHAP (SHapley Additive exPlanations)**: SHAP values provide a unified measure of feature importance by calculating the contribution of each feature to the model's prediction. SHAP is

especially useful for tree-based models like **XGBoost** and **Random Forests**.

3. **Surrogate Models**: Surrogate models involve training a simpler, interpretable model (like a decision tree) on the predictions of a complex model. This can provide insight into the complex model's behavior while maintaining interpretability.

Real-World Examples: Biased Facial Recognition Systems and Credit Scoring Controversies

1. Biased Facial Recognition Systems:

Facial recognition technology has gained widespread adoption in applications like security, law enforcement, and even retail. However, these systems have been shown to exhibit significant **racial biases**, often misidentifying people of color, especially Black and Asian individuals, at much higher rates than white individuals.

- **Example**: A 2018 study by the **National Institute of Standards and Technology (NIST)** found that commercial facial recognition systems were more likely to misidentify people with darker skin tones and women. This has led to concerns about the use of facial recognition in sensitive areas, such as law enforcement and hiring decisions, where biased misidentification could result in unfair outcomes.

2. Credit Scoring Controversies:

Credit scoring systems are another area where AI can have unintended consequences. These systems are used to determine an individual's creditworthiness, which affects their ability to obtain loans, mortgages, or credit cards. However, traditional credit scoring models often rely on historical data that may contain inherent biases, leading to discrimination against certain demographic groups.

- **Example:** In the U.S., it has been found that credit scoring models disproportionately affect minority communities, particularly Black and Hispanic individuals, by giving them lower scores based on factors such as zip codes, which can correlate with socioeconomic status.

Actionable Advice: Checklists for Ensuring Fairness

To help mitigate bias and ensure that AI models are ethical, fair, and responsible, it's essential to adopt a systematic approach. Here are some **checklists** that can guide you through the process:

1. Data Collection and Preparation:

- Ensure that the dataset is **representative** of the population.

- Check for **imbalance** in the dataset, particularly in sensitive attributes like gender, race, and age.

- Remove **biased** or sensitive information that could unintentionally influence model outcomes.

- Ensure that data used for training is **clean**, with no missing or erroneous values.

2. Model Development:

- Regularly test for **bias** in model predictions across different demographic groups.

- Use **fairness metrics** like **demographic parity, equalized odds**, and **disparate impact** to evaluate model fairness.

- Incorporate **explainability** techniques such as **LIME** and **SHAP** to ensure transparency in model decision-making.

3. Model Evaluation and Deployment:

- Conduct an **ethical review** to assess potential risks of model deployment, including privacy, fairness, and transparency concerns.

- Ensure the model performs well across all subgroups and **does not discriminate**.

- Monitor the model after deployment to ensure it continues to perform fairly and remains aligned with ethical standards.

Hands-On Project: Perform a Bias Check on a Classification Dataset

For this hands-on project, we'll work through a case study that involves checking for **bias** in a classification dataset. We will use a publicly available dataset and measure differences in accuracy between subgroups, such as gender, race, or other sensitive attributes. We'll then explore potential fixes for any observed bias.

Step 1: Load the Dataset

We will use the **Adult Income** dataset from the UCI Machine Learning Repository, which contains demographic information like age, education, and gender, and is used to predict whether a person earns more than $50K per year.

python

```python
import pandas as pd

from sklearn.model_selection import train_test_split


# Load the Adult Income dataset

data = pd.read_csv('adult.csv')


# Split the data into features and target variable

X = data.drop('income', axis=1)

y = data['income']
```

Split into training and testing sets

X_train, X_test, y_train, y_test = train_test_split(X, y, test_size=0.2, random_state=42)

Step 2: Train the Model

We'll train a simple **Logistic Regression** model to predict income.

python

```
from sklearn.linear_model import LogisticRegression

from sklearn.metrics import accuracy_score


# Train a logistic regression model

model = LogisticRegression(max_iter=1000)

model.fit(X_train, y_train)


# Evaluate the model

y_pred = model.predict(X_test)
```

accuracy = accuracy_score(y_test, y_pred)

print(f"Accuracy: {accuracy}")

Step 3: Check for Bias in Subgroups

We will check the accuracy of the model for different subgroups, such as gender and race.

python

```
# Check accuracy for different gender groups

accuracy_male = accuracy_score(y_test[X_test['gender'] ==
'Male'], y_pred[X_test['gender'] == 'Male'])

accuracy_female = accuracy_score(y_test[X_test['gender'] ==
'Female'], y_pred[X_test['gender'] == 'Female'])


print(f"Accuracy for males: {accuracy_male}")

print(f"Accuracy for females: {accuracy_female}")
```

Step 4: Mitigate Bias

If we find disparities in accuracy between groups, we can try several fixes, such as:

- **Resampling** the data to ensure equal representation of different groups.

- **Re-weighting** the training examples to give more importance to underrepresented groups.

- **Fairness constraints** during model training to enforce equal accuracy across groups.

Conclusion

In this chapter, we've explored the ethical considerations surrounding machine learning, focusing on issues such as **bias, privacy, data security**, and **model transparency**. We discussed how **machine learning** models can perpetuate or exacerbate biases if not carefully managed and provided practical steps for **mitigating bias** in datasets and models.

Through real-world examples like **biased facial recognition systems** and **credit scoring controversies**, we illustrated the importance of building responsible AI systems that are fair, transparent, and accountable. We also provided actionable checklists for ensuring fairness in data collection, model development, and deployment.

Finally, through the hands-on project, we demonstrated how to check for bias in a classification dataset and explore potential fixes. By applying these principles, you can build AI systems that not only perform well but also respect ethical guidelines and contribute to a more just and equitable society.

Chapter 15: Looking Ahead – Trends, Resources, and Next Steps

Introduction

Machine learning (ML) has evolved rapidly over the last decade, and its impact on industries, technology, and everyday life continues to grow. As we've explored throughout this book, machine learning is already transforming sectors like healthcare, manufacturing, logistics, and more. But even with all the advancements we've seen, the field is far from static. The future of machine learning holds exciting possibilities—new techniques, tools, and resources that can make machine learning more accessible, efficient, and impactful.

In this final chapter, we will look ahead to **emerging trends** in machine learning, such as **AutoML, edge computing**, and **federated learning**. We'll also discuss how you can **continue your learning journey**, pointing you toward valuable resources like datasets, online communities, and competitions (e.g., Kaggle). Most importantly, we'll encourage you to take what you've learned and apply it to projects in domains you're passionate about, showing how to develop a **mini end-to-end machine learning project**.

By the end of this chapter, you'll have the tools to keep learning and exploring machine learning on your own, whether you're looking to build more complex models, dive into new trends, or contribute to the growing AI community.

The Future of Machine Learning: AutoML, Edge Computing, and Federated Learning

Machine learning is advancing at an astonishing pace, and new trends are shaping the future of how we develop and deploy models. Below are some of the most exciting trends to watch.

1. AutoML – Democratizing Machine Learning

AutoML (Automated Machine Learning) is revolutionizing the way machine learning models are built. Traditionally, building an ML model involves several steps—data preprocessing, feature engineering, model selection, hyperparameter tuning, and evaluation. These steps require significant expertise and time.

AutoML seeks to automate much of this process, making it easier for non-experts to build high-quality models and for experts to focus on more strategic tasks. The goal of AutoML is to streamline the process of applying machine learning to real-world problems, reducing the barrier to entry for ML practitioners.

- **What AutoML Does**: AutoML platforms automate various stages of the machine learning workflow, including data preprocessing, model selection, feature engineering, and hyperparameter optimization. This can be done with minimal input from the user, who simply provides the data and defines the problem.

- **Popular AutoML Tools**:

    - **Google Cloud AutoML**: A suite of machine learning products that allow users to train custom models with minimal coding.

    - **H2O.ai**: Offers an open-source AutoML platform that automates model training and tuning.

    - **TPOT** and **Auto-sklearn**: Python-based AutoML libraries that optimize machine learning pipelines using evolutionary algorithms.

- **Impact**: AutoML lowers the barriers for entry into the field of machine learning, enabling a broader range of professionals (including business analysts, marketers, and others without extensive coding backgrounds) to develop useful ML models. However, it also accelerates the pace of innovation by enabling quicker iterations and deployments of ML solutions.

2. Edge Computing – Bringing ML Closer to the Source

Edge computing involves performing computation on devices close to where data is generated, rather than relying on a central server or cloud. This trend is particularly important for applications that need real-time processing or have limited connectivity to centralized data centers.

- **What Edge Computing Does**: Edge computing allows machine learning models to run on devices like smartphones, IoT devices, or autonomous vehicles. Instead of sending data to the cloud for processing, the data is processed locally on the device, reducing latency and bandwidth usage.

- **Real-World Applications**:

  - **Autonomous vehicles**: Cars equipped with edge computing devices can process data from cameras, radar, and sensors in real-time to make immediate decisions.

- o **Smartphones**: Many modern smartphones now run machine learning models directly on the device, enabling real-time features such as face recognition and voice assistants.

- **Impact**: Edge computing improves performance by enabling real-time processing and reduces the dependency on cloud infrastructure, making it ideal for applications in remote or mobile environments.

3. Federated Learning – Decentralized Collaboration

Federated learning is an approach to training machine learning models in a distributed manner. Instead of gathering data from various sources and sending it to a central server, federated learning allows models to be trained locally on devices (e.g., smartphones or edge devices) while keeping data decentralized.

- **What Federated Learning Does**: Federated learning allows machine learning models to be trained on decentralized data while keeping that data on the devices themselves. The model training happens on each device, and only model updates are shared, not raw data.

- **Real-World Applications**:

  - **Google's Gboard**: The Google keyboard uses federated learning to personalize typing suggestions without transmitting your private data to Google's servers.

  - **Healthcare**: Federated learning could enable medical institutions to collaborate on training models for disease prediction or drug discovery, while keeping patient data secure and private.

- **Impact**: Federated learning makes it possible to train powerful machine learning models without compromising user privacy. It ensures that sensitive data stays on local devices and is never centralized, making it ideal for privacy-sensitive applications.

Continuous Learning: Finding Datasets, Communities, and Competitions

The field of machine learning is constantly evolving, and staying up to date is essential. Fortunately, there are a wealth of resources to help you continue learning, improve your skills, and get involved in the community.

1. Finding Datasets

Datasets are the backbone of any machine learning project. Finding high-quality, relevant data is essential for building effective models.

- **Kaggle**: Kaggle is one of the most popular platforms for data science and machine learning. It provides access to thousands of datasets, ranging from beginner-level projects to highly complex datasets for advanced research.

- **UCI Machine Learning Repository**: The UCI repository is a classic resource for machine learning datasets, including everything from healthcare data to customer behavior.

- **Google Dataset Search**: Google's Dataset Search tool helps you find datasets hosted across various repositories, universities, and organizations worldwide.

- **Open Data Portals**: Many governments and organizations provide open access to datasets. Platforms like **data.gov** (U.S.) and **EU Open Data Portal** are excellent sources of open datasets.

2. Joining ML Communities

Machine learning is a dynamic field, and connecting with others can help you stay on top of the latest trends, discover new resources, and find collaborators.

- **Kaggle**: In addition to datasets, Kaggle is home to one of the largest data science communities. Participate in competitions, share code, and learn from top practitioners around the world.

- **Reddit (r/MachineLearning)**: The **r/MachineLearning** subreddit is a great place to discuss the latest research, share tutorials, and ask questions.

- **Stack Overflow**: The **Machine Learning** tag on Stack Overflow is filled with developers and data scientists who can help troubleshoot your ML challenges.

- **Meetups and Conferences**: Attend meetups and conferences, such as **NeurIPS, ICML**, and **CVPR**, to network with experts, learn from industry leaders, and stay current on the latest research and trends.

3. Participating in ML Competitions

Competitions are a fantastic way to sharpen your skills, apply what you've learned, and tackle real-world problems.

- **Kaggle Competitions**: Kaggle is home to some of the most well-known data science competitions, where you can compete against the world's best data scientists to solve problems in fields ranging from computer vision to natural language processing.

- **DrivenData**: DrivenData hosts competitions focused on social good, where you can apply your ML skills to solve problems like disease prediction, environmental conservation, and education.

- **Zindi**: Zindi hosts AI competitions focused on solving challenges in Africa, providing a unique opportunity to engage with problems relevant to the African continent.

Encouraging Curiosity-Driven Exploration Beyond the Book

This book has provided a comprehensive foundation for your journey into machine learning. However, machine learning is an incredibly vast field, and the learning doesn't stop here. Curiosity-driven exploration is one of the most important aspects of mastering ML, as the field is constantly evolving with new techniques, tools, and applications.

- **Stay Curious**: Continuously seek out new challenges, whether they involve solving a specific problem in a domain you're passionate about, experimenting with cutting-edge models, or diving deeper into mathematical concepts.

- **Cross-Disciplinary Learning**: ML is applied across many domains, including **healthcare, finance, robotics**, and **artificial intelligence ethics**. Exploring these fields and understanding how ML intersects with them will deepen your understanding and open up new opportunities.

- **Research Papers and Journals**: Reading research papers is essential for staying on the cutting edge. Start with **arXiv.org** for access to the latest machine learning research, and consider subscribing to journals like **The Journal of Machine Learning Research**.

Practical Wrap-Up: The Essential Toolkit

As you continue your machine learning journey, it's important to have a set of tools and resources that you can rely on. Here's a summary of the essential tools you'll use in the field:

1. Libraries and Frameworks:

- **TensorFlow/Keras**: For building deep learning models.

- **PyTorch**: An alternative deep learning framework known for its flexibility and ease of use.

- **scikit-learn**: A library for traditional machine learning algorithms like regression, classification, and clustering.

- **XGBoost**: A powerful gradient boosting library for structured data tasks.

- **Pandas**: For data manipulation and analysis.

- **Matplotlib/Seaborn**: For data visualization.

2. Platforms:

- **Kaggle**: For datasets, competitions, and community engagement.

- **Google Colab**: For cloud-based Jupyter notebooks with free GPU access.

- **GitHub**: For sharing code and collaborating on projects.

- **AWS SageMaker**: For end-to-end ML model development, from training to deployment.

3. Tools for Deployment:

- **Flask/Django**: For deploying models as web services.

- **Docker**: For containerizing ML models to ensure portability and scalability.

- **TensorFlow Lite/ONNX**: For deploying models to mobile devices and edge devices.

Final Hands-On Challenge: Design a Mini End-to-End ML Project

Now that you've gained a solid foundation, it's time to put everything you've learned into practice. For this challenge, pick a domain that excites you—whether it's healthcare, sports, social media, or even something creative like art or music—and design a **mini end-to-end ML project**. Here are the general steps:

1. Define the Problem

- Choose a domain that interests you. For example, if you're interested in sports, you might predict the performance of a player based on their historical data.

- Define the specific problem you want to solve (e.g., "Predict the next day's temperature," or "Classify whether a tweet is positive or negative").

2. Collect Data

- Look for publicly available datasets that fit your problem. You can use platforms like **Kaggle**, **UCI Machine Learning Repository**, or **Google Dataset Search**.

- If data is not readily available, consider using web scraping techniques or APIs to gather the necessary data.

3. Data Cleaning and Preprocessing

- Clean the data by handling missing values, removing duplicates, and transforming variables.

- Normalize or standardize numerical features, and perform any necessary feature engineering.

4. Model Selection

- Select an appropriate model for your problem. For classification, you might use **Logistic Regression**, **Random Forests**, or **Neural Networks**. For time series, you could explore **ARIMA** or **LSTM**.

5. Train the Model

- Split the data into training and testing sets.

- Train the model on the training data, and tune the hyperparameters to optimize performance.

6. Evaluate the Model

- Evaluate the model on the test set using appropriate metrics (accuracy, precision, recall, etc.).

- If performance is not satisfactory, consider tuning the model or exploring additional features.

7. Deployment

- Deploy your model as a simple web app using **Flask** or **Streamlit**.

- Alternatively, package the model into a script that can be run locally or from a cloud service.

8. Share and Reflect

- Share your project on **GitHub** or **Kaggle**.

- Reflect on the lessons learned throughout the project and areas for improvement.

Conclusion

Machine learning is a rapidly evolving field with limitless potential, and this chapter has equipped you with the resources and frameworks you need to continue your journey. We've covered key trends like **AutoML, edge computing**, and **federated learning**, and provided guidance on how to stay engaged with the community, explore datasets, and participate in competitions.

With the hands-on challenge, you've learned how to take a project from start to finish, defining the problem, collecting data, building and evaluating models, and deploying your solution. Remember, the best way to continue growing in machine learning is through continuous learning, exploration, and practice.

www.ingramcontent.com/pod-product-compliance
Lightning Source LLC
LaVergne TN
LVHW022338060326
832902LV00022B/4103